Memoirs
of an Antique Dealer

Written by
Frank Hicks

Published by
F. Hicks Publishing
Hudson, Quebec, Canada
450-458-0385

Printed by
Clò Communications
Hudson, Quebec, Canada
514-265-2656
www.clocommunications.com

ISBN 978-1-9767499-7-1

I've given many lectures over the years on the subject of antiques and collectibles. After every one, a number of the older people in the audience would approach me, lamenting, "If only I had heard this lecture before I emptied out my home." Like the cavalry in the old movies I always arrived too late.

Hopefully, this book will correct my timing problem — and some readers will avoid costly errors and benefit from my experiences.

The stories in this book are all true. Names and locations have been changed to protect the privacy of those concerned and time sequences might differ a bit because of my aging memory.

Some sections of this book might offend people. The language I use is not always recommended in polite society. Rewriting history to accommodate the reader is not something I recommend.

I would like to thank all the friends who pushed me to write this book and my wife who has put up for the last 30 years with this crazy, introspective Irishman with the self-effacing sense of humour. She would have gotten less time for killing me.

My thanks also go out to Kels (Kelley) Deegan for her wonderful photographs, Quebec artist René Lalonde for his amazing cover art, Janet Mann as well as my old friend Sinik for their amazing cartoons, and all the colourful customers throughout the years who supplied me with my stories.

WARNING

This book contains strong language, implied sexual situations and disturbing insights into the human psyche.

It also contains passages that politically correct and holier-than- thou readers may find disturbing.

Reader discretion is advised.

The opinions and situations expressed in this publication do not necessarily reflect the views of anyone other than the author.

The stories are all true, the names have been changed to protect the guilty as well as the innocent.

Not wishing to waste the reader's time or money I endeavored to write an introduction that would truly capture the essence and intent of my book. All my attempts failed in comparison to this simple yet honest letter from an editorial friend of mine.

Dear Frank

I'm about to head out to the country for about a week, but before leaving, I wanted to let you know that I finished reading your book. At first, I wasn't sure I'd be able to personally connect with your experiences in the antique and collectibles business, since that world is so foreign to me, much as I love beautiful antiques. But as I was reading it, I became utterly fascinated by the parade of interesting people that you met in the course of your 30 years as an antique dealer. Their often tragicomic stories reflected the nature of the human condition so well that I found myself relating very well to their own experiences, and to yours too, as you tried to understand what made them act, think, and react the way they did to the various things that life had in store for them. I really enjoyed how you leavened your keen observations about these various "characters" -- including the animals -- with your trademark wry humour that often borders on the irreverent and even profane. But throughout it all, you "called it as you saw it," even when your unvarnished honesty demanded the kind of vocabulary I last heard uttered by teenage boys slumped at the back of the 211 bus on a Saturday night. I also loved the stories about Marilyn's unstoppable animal rescue efforts that invariably lassoed you in as much as they did the animals. And of course our dearly departed Shanon is now immortalized forever as he and Benny continue to play tug-of-war with your guest's designer jacket.

What a remarkable and memorable portrait of your life you've painted for yourself and your readers, Frank. What a better understanding you must have of your own life's journey as you look back on these last 30 years of your life in the antique-and-story-collecting business.

I've gotta get back to my packing now, but thanks for writing such an engaging book!----Best Wishes

Lisa

Contents

*Dedicated to
my loving wife,
Marilyn*

Starting up in business

I started my career as a buyer and seller of other people's junk in an offbeat, tongue-in-cheek sort of way. It was back during the great recession of 1982 and I was working as a financial controller for a small engineering firm.

A bunch of the boys asked me out to lunch at the local watering hole where the beer was cold and the food was edible. While enjoying our usual meal of underdone steaks and overdone meatloaf washed down with an ice-cold draft beer, we started chewing the fat, literally and figuratively, on the usual subjects of politics, sports and sex when the subject of the state of the economy came up.

We were going through a tough recession and everyone was concerned about his job. Wiping beer foam from his lips, Steve, the technical manager, turned to me and asked, "Frank, what business would you recommend opening during this recession?" In my semi-drunken stupor, I replied, "The junk business, of course. Everyone has junk they want to get rid of and everyone wants someone else's junk. The circle is endless. You're buying cheap at one end and selling cheap at the other, but there's a healthy profit margin in the middle. Everybody wins, nobody loses. The business is recession-proof, the harder the times the better the business."

I suggested a good name for the business would be, Hard Times, borrowed from Charles Dickens. The other name proposed, Other Peoples Crap Inc., was roundly rejected. We all had a good laugh and went on to the more interesting topics of hockey, football, baseball and sex.

After lunch I went back to my office and returned to the job of counting other people's money, projecting other people's profits and trimming other people's costs.

Later that afternoon Steve came into my office, put his feet up on my desk and said, "Frank, that idea of yours is not as stupid as it sounds," to which I quickly replied, "What idea, and get your feet off my desk."

"Why, the second-hand business of course," he said. "If I find a store, will you go partners with me?" I told him that I would have to think about it and would get back to him.

That night I brought the subject up with my wife Marilyn and she thought it was a great idea as long as I held on to my job as backup. She had recently lost her job so she offered to work free of charge. Steve found a small shop located inside an apartment building on a busy commercial street. The rent was $600 a month and we signed a two-year lease. We started out with a bank account of $2,000. Steve's wife, Monique, offered her services as well so we now had a shop and the staff to work it. We used what little start-up money we had on second-hand shelves, a cash register and a new outdoor sign. Start-up stock consisted of items supplied by friends and relatives on a consignment basis.

Our cheap wine and cheese opening day extravaganza produced $1,200 in sales. We were flying! My wife began believing she might even one day receive a salary but then things began to slow down after the opening. Monique and Marilyn took turns watching the shop. In time, people on the street started to know us. I soon realized that we couldn't continue to depend on the cast-offs of friends and family so I started searching the papers for classified ads and hitting every moving, estate, and garage sale I could fit into my schedule. It's surprising what you can find once you tap into the amazing and assorted reserves of second-hand goods in this city. Every Saturday morning I would drag myself out of bed at 6 a.m., and head out on the road in my trusty car with a few hundred dollars in my pocket. I was treasure hunting, not underground or deep in the depths of the ocean but in the garages and driveways of NDG, Westmount, and Montreal West. After a few months of garage sale shopping, I found it difficult to go into a retail store and pay retail prices. I was paying $2 for a pair of jeans that would cost me $50 retail and $1 for a tie that would normally cost me $20. At the garage sale, they threw a belt into the bargain. These might have been small treasures, but they felt good. Some treasures were not all that small, like the early 19th century Prussian sword or the 18th century duelling pistol, or the 11th century framed page of Gregorian chants. Steve or I would keep some of the treasures we bought for ourselves but most would end up in the shop at what we later discovered were, ridiculously low prices. Our lack of antiques and collectibles knowledge was costing us money but the store was filling up and I was having fun.

After the first year of operation, Steve asked me to buy him out at his initial investment. He was a rather shy guy and had difficulty dealing with people on a one-to-one basis. He was also having some marriage problems, so I sadly said goodbye and returned his thousand dollar start-up money.

I was now the one hundred percent owner of Hard Times.

Building the business

Now that the business was mine, the first item on the agenda was providing a salary for Marilyn. My good looks and wild bedroom antics alone were no longer enough. Working in any store can be rewarding and stressful at times. Working in a second-hand store cranks the stress level up substantially. Many wonderful and interesting customers came into our lives but we also had our share of exasperating characters. The asshole factor, as I referred to it, had to be built-in when deciding what would be a fair wage.

We finally came to an amount we both could agree on and I tackled the next problem. I called the landlord and scheduled a meeting. Over coffee at a local restaurant, he agreed to a new five-year lease with a five-year renewable option and his promise to install a commercial front door. The next step was to purchase an antique store counter at a going-out-of-business sale. With my new door installed and a new counter in place our little store was starting to look somewhat respectable.

My car was too small for the pick-up work so I bought a second hand Datsun station wagon at a garage sale for $100. It was a little rusty but ran like a charm and had lots of room in the back to transport junk and treasures.

Over the next year, the stock in our shop consisted of everything from stuffed cobras, unicycles, fur coats, records, toys, books, dishes and the occasional kitchen sink. Calls came in daily from people offering to buy or sell items. Most of the calls were the normal everyday variety but a few were bizarre and some were sad. A woman called and asked if I was interested in purchasing a solid gold intrauterine coil (IUD). I politely refused, stating that I was not in the practice of buying scrap gold and doubted if anyone would want a second-hand birth control device even if it *was* made of gold. "It might make an attractive pendant for around the neck," I said. A couple of days later I get another call asking if I had any used women's underwear for sale. I told the caller I couldn't keep up with the demand for that particular item but I still had a few pairs of my old shorts that I would gladly sell him at a greatly reduced price. Unfortunately, he didn't see the humor in my offer and rudely slammed the phone in my ear. I never heard from him again. Those calls always gave Marilyn and me a good laugh and we just wrote them off to the full moon syndrome.

Some calls were disturbing. Two days before Christmas, Marilyn received a call from a young woman wanting to sell some items. After my day at the office (I still had my regular job) I headed over to the address given to see what she had to offer. An attractive young woman answered the door and brought me into the bedroom of her modest 3 ½ room apartment. I was feeling very uncomfortable. In the corner of this sparsely-furnished room I noticed a crib with a small child sleeping, arms wrapped tightly around a teddy bear. The young woman told me that her husband had abandoned her and the child and she was waiting for her first welfare check. The only items she had of any value were the child's toys and she was wondering if I would be interested in buying them. Being in the junk business for over a year now, I believed I knew a scam when I heard one. This was no scam. I told her the toys were of no use to me but I would give her some money to help her get past the holidays. When Marilyn heard what I had done she insisted we go to the local grocery store, get an order of food and household supplies and drop it off at the young woman's apartment. After the holidays were over, she came to thank Marilyn and me and to tell us about her wonderful Christmas.

Approximately three months later this same young woman turns up at the store stating that she was short rent money and asking if I could lend her two hundred dollars. My bullshit antenna was sending out warning signals, but ignoring them I lent her the money anyway.

I never saw her again.

Leaving my job

The business card proclaiming Frank Hicks Financial Controller & part time junk dealer would soon be radically changed. The CEO of the engineering company I worked for had a unique concept on how to run a successful business. He went by the "Field Of Dreams" method of business development. His version of, "IF YOU BUILD IT THEY WILL COME," was, "IF YOU BILL IT THEY WILL PAY." The fact that we had no purchase orders for the work and that completed invoices were never sent to the client meant nothing to this man. Every month this CEO would tell me to process a large billing to client XYZ. This client was a European engineering firm that had developed a garbage recycling process that sorted garbage and turned it into building materials. The CEO's plan was to partner with this firm in building the first plant of this kind in North America. All the work done and expenses incurred by our firm would then go towards our equity in this new joint venture. The fact that we hadn't yet tied down any municipal contracts to process garbage and that there were a number of other obstacles in our way meant nothing to this CEO. He knew what he was doing and you'd better not stand in his way.

I struggled to make payroll every two weeks and spent my days fighting off creditors while he went on fancy company trips and charged expensive meals and fancy jewelry to the company. The little second-hand recycling business I was doing on the side was generating more real profit than this CEO's fancy recycling dream. The company was getting deeper and deeper into debt with the bank. One day I was instructed to sign the company's financial statements and receivable listing and present the signed reports to our bank manager as support for our cash position. I refused, stating that the reports were based on invoices that I was forced to produce but could not honestly support. I was told that I could either sign the reports and deliver them to the bank or submit my resignation. I turned to the CEO and said, "I'm sorry, sir, but you leave me no choice but to submit my AMF."

"What the hell is an AMF?" he asked.

"Adios, Mother Fucker," I replied as I walked out the door.

Not long after, this engineering company went bankrupt.

Now the work starts

I had taken the bold step of leaving my employment with the WICKED ENGINEER OF THE WEST and now had to survive on my wits and intelligence alone. I figured I was in deep doo-doo. Marilyn had a different view.

She was optimistic about our future and excited about starting a new and challenging life. Her enthusiasm was contagious so we went out and bought ourselves a new-old home with lots of garage and basement storage space. We then purchased a new Dodge Ram pick-up truck. I was now a certified Junk Dealer.

I wasn't really certified by any organization of junk dealers but I was definitely certifiable. When the rest of my family heard what I had done, they started to seriously question my sanity and their gene pool. My sister Susie wanted to know if she would go crazy one day like her older brother. I assured them that I knew exactly what I was doing and that everything would work out great. Now that I convinced them, I had to convince myself. I attacked the classified ads in the paper every morning in my unending quest for treasure. I discovered that there is an art to hunting for treasure. Deep sea divers study charts and maps to learn where the treasure is, try to beat the other treasure hunters to the site and then have the ability to recognize the crustaceous artifacts on the ocean floor as treasures. I had to take a similar approach.

During the week, I would study the classified ads and plot out my course for the day. I would head out every morning and try to beat the pickers to the prizes. Pickers are freelance treasure-hunters who race to every moving, clean up, and estate sale listed in the paper. They grab anything they consider saleable and inexpensive and then flog their wares to the antique or collectible dealers ready to pay their price. Today, they also have the option of logging onto the internet and selling on E-Bay, Craig's List, and numerous other web sites.

When I arrived at a house or apartment indicated in a classified listing, I would check out the items being sold, make my selection and negotiate the price. After closing the deal, I would load up my booty and race on to the next location attempting to arrive before the competition. When the possibility of arriving at virgin territory became unlikely, I called it a day and headed back to the shop. After unloading all the stock, Marilyn and I would price, shelve, and hopefully sell the merchandise. It's in this final phase of operations that I usually screwed up.

The seasoned oceanic treasure-hunter recognizes the crustaceous artifacts as treasure. I didn't. The number of precious antiques and collectibles that I undersold in my early days is something I don't like to dwell on. I had a good eye for quality; I just didn't have the knowledge to go along with that instinctive eye.

One good example of this was the time I purchased a trunk full of dolls and decided to give one to Marilyn as a birthday gift. After picking what I considered the best of the bunch and wrapping it beautifully, I presented it to Marilyn. My gift went over like flatulence at a feast. She said it reminded her of the killer doll named Chucky in the movie "Child's Play." One night an antique dealer was at our home and noticed the doll. He offered my wife five hundred dollars for it and, ignoring my protests, she accepted. Years later we discovered the doll was worth over ten thousand dollars. She never questioned my judgment again.

In the early days, antique dealers and pickers would show up at my store daily hoping to cash in on one of my mistakes.

About half a block from my store there was an antique store run by two characters named Albert and Manat. Albert spent most of his time in the shop or on the road so I didn't see much of him. Five foot eight, three hundred ninety pounds, baby-faced, butter wouldn't melt in his mouth, Manat was another story. He would come into my shop once or twice a day checking for mistakes. If he found something, he would always say, "I think I'll buy this for my aunt" (or sister or mother or niece). Personally, I doubted he had any family at all and if he did I'm sure they weren't talking to him. No matter how under-priced the piece was, it was always too expensive for Manat. He always wanted a better price.

One day he purchased a beautiful Victorian bird-in-a-cage, automaton for fifteen dollars. The asking price for the piece was twenty dollars, but of course it was too expensive for Manatee, sorry I mean Manat. He told Marilyn he only wanted something small for his niece and couldn't pay over fifteen dollars.

Two weeks later I see the same automaton in a high-end antique shop window selling for five hundred and ninety five dollars. From that day forward, I watched every item he purchased and held firmly to my price. I was leaving way too much money on the table. I had to get smart fast.

Learning the ropes

Back in the early days, there was no Antique Road Show or Internet to refer to. I had to learn the hard way. I started attending antique shows, auctions and flea markets. I visited antique shops around the city checking out the stock and asking the prices of items. Little by little, it was beginning to sink in.

My store was still selling the nearly-new irons, toasters, frying pans and everything else under the sun. These items helped pay my everyday expenses and Marilyn's salary but it was the antiques and collectibles that generated the real profit. I began to know the professional dealers who frequented the shop and closely watched their buying habits. It was a learning experience that was eye-opening and sometimes, eye-popping. I started spending money on antique price guides. Books like Kovels' and Miller's became my bibles and my daily companions.

I discovered that there were books published on every collectible possible. Books on everything from fountain pens to marbles were all easily available in bookstores and libraries. There were books on books. I still made mistakes but I was making fewer and fewer of them and they were not costing me as much.

I came to realize that the world of antiques and collectibles was a far-reaching and somewhat bizarre world comprising many wonderful and interesting people. It also had its share of fakes and charlatans. Many people call themselves antique experts but, then again, many people call themselves Napoleon Bonaparte. The same credibility factor applies to both.

The world of antiques and collectibles consisted of so many different categories of items with so many factors affecting their value that it was hard to avoid making mistakes.

Knowledge equalled cash benefits in this business. The more you knew, the more you grew. I read about the knowledgeable antique dealer who sold a self-published pamphlet entitled "Tamerlane and Other Poems," by 'A Bostonian' for fifteen dollars and later discovered that the pamphlet known to book collectors as "The Black Tulip", written by Edgar Allan Poe, was worth close to two hundred thousand dollars. I read about the Philadelphia Chippendale Mahogany card table that sold at one auction for a little over one thousand dollars and then sold twelve days later for over one million dollars. I knew I had made mistakes. I just hoped that they weren't that big.

Over time, I got to know my customers' likes and dislikes and on my various buying trips around town I would acquire items for specific customers. The goal was to purchase a number of items and get an immediate payback by selling a small portion of those new purchases, leaving the rest free on board.

People from every walk of life would visit the shop. The moderately rich shopped side-by-side with the poor. They all came looking for bargains. I did my best to make sure they left the shop smiling. Sometimes I was successful and sometimes not. If a product was proven defective, I would return the client's money immediately believing it was more important to have a client for life than an unsatisfied one-time customer. Marilyn warned me to always keep the lid screwed tight on my hot Irish temper and I usually succeeded— usually, but not always. One time she sold a hair dryer to a young mentally-challanged couple for three dollars. She would have gladly given them the dryer but didn't want them to feel they were being treated differently from other customers. They left the store happy with their new purchase. About an hour later, a male welfare agent comes into the store with the dryer screaming about it being defective. Bouncing it off, and almost breaking, my glass counter he asks, "How dare you take advantage of a mentally-challenged couple?" Before my wife could stop me, I flew around the counter, grabbed the welfare agent by the scuff of the neck and carried him to the front door. Once outside I held him over a spiked fence and enlightened him on the proper way to return a defective item without getting yourself killed. Retreating to my counter, I waited quietly as he returned and informed me in a polite and peaceful manner that the dryer was defective. I plugged it in, checked it out, verified that it was indeed defective and remitted the money apologizing for any inconvenience I might have caused. As he was walked out of the store, I said, "Now, wasn't that a lot easier?" Marilyn just looked over at me, shaking her head.

My Old Curiosity Shop - By Frank Hicks

A shop full of memories
of bygone times
when craftsmanship and pride of work
where not just marketing clichés

A shop full of memories
preserved lovingly
until hardship, necessity, disillusionment or death
passed them on

A shop full of memories
where history is recaptured-made fresh
touched lovingly with caring hands
where young minds are opened

A shop full of memories
recalling the days of our youth
loving artifacts of those we loved
and those that loved us.

The art of garage sale shopping

I discovered that there was an art to garage sale shopping. Every Thursday and Friday, I would check out the local papers and make a listing of all the garage sales in my surrounding area. The area was full of old, interesting homes so I knew it was prime treasure-hunting territory. My garage sale listing would indicate the location, opening and closing times and any other information I considered pertinent. Were antiques and collectibles listed in the sale? Were early birds forbidden? Was it classified as an estate or moving sale? Was it a multi-family or street sale? Is this the first sale at the residence or have they had other sales? After reviewing my listing, I would then prioritize it and plot out my route for the following day. The strategy was to get to the most garage sales in the least amount of time. Doddering about aimlessly was not an option. The window of opportunity was small, so I had to strike hard and fast. If the sale was opening at eight I had to be there by seven. A lot of my competitors would go to the sales days in advance. Many went very early in the morning, ringing bells and dragging people from their beds. I like to believe that I was never hungry or greedy enough to resort to such drastic action. Maybe I just lacked the nerve or my fragile ego couldn't take doors being slammed in my face. I missed out on a lot of interesting and profitable items. But, on the other hand, I didn't end up with a bruised and broken nose.

If only the sellers realized that the first items sold are always the most desirable. Allowing rude and inconsiderate dealers the first choice encourages their bad behaviour and usually ends up getting the seller a lower price.

Most sellers start setting up an hour before the published opening time and will let you shop if you show up. Some would insist they would only open at the specified time. Thanking them, I would drive away just to return fifteen minutes before opening time and find twenty cars parked outside the property and people walking away with their purchases — so much for NO EARLY BIRDS.

Once at the garage sale, I looked around quickly, there was no time to waste. When all I discovered was junk, I cut my losses, jumped in my truck and headed off to the next one. If a treasure or two was found, I would hold on to them closely, start the bargaining process, pay the seller and head out again. The later in the day, the better the discount that could be negotiated, but as time went up quality usually went down.

When a treasure is found it's always advisable to ask the seller if he or she has any other items for sale that are not on display. At a really good garage sale, the dealers and non-dealers alike would pick up any items they considered interesting and set them aside in their own little selected area on the lawn to keep the treasures away from envious eyes and competitors. Bulk buying usually resulted in lower overall prices. I remember one garage sale I arrived at and noticed a flea market dealer that had lined up five beautiful oak-enclosed 19th century brass scientific instruments valued at about $5,000 on his little corner of the lawn. As I was passing, I heard him calling the seller over and asking a group price. She said seventy five dollars and he offered fifty. She accepted and my heart skipped a beat. What galled me, aside from the fact that I missed out on a great deal, was the knowledge that the dealer knew the deal was amazing at the asking price but he just couldn't help turning the screw so much tighter.

Fun, fuck-ups and frustrations

No matter what the occasion I couldn't let anything interfere with my Saturday 7 to 10 a.m. garage sale time. Heading out early, my truck would always be overloaded by the time I returned to the house where I would unload and head out again. On a good Saturday, I would make three trips. Sunday was usually a day of rest but I couldn't help running to one or two Sunday sales. The rest of my week was spent racing to moving sales, placing and pricing stock and selling and buying goods over the counter. My life had turned into a swap meet and I loved every minute of it. Our shop attracted an interesting assortment of regular customers. Every personality type and personality disorder eventually showed up at my door. Many customers came in just to unload their emotional burdens and I was a good listener. We had interesting and important debates on politics, religion, the state of the world and which liquorice was better, the black or the red. I chose the red because I was told black liquorice made your stool green and that didn't sound good. I often took the opposing view on any debates, just for the pure hell of it. Not only did I have an interesting variety of customers, I also had an interesting variety of employees.

Ted Daton, a part-time actor and voice-over man would come in regularly to pass the time. We became good friends and Ted would tell me about all the projects he was working on. Ted would go into a sound studio in the morning to do multiple voices for cartoon characters for a Saturday morning children's show. In the afternoon he headed over to a second sound studio where he would supply the sound effects for adult triple x-rated films. Being a method actor Ted would act out all the parts while seated in his sound booth. He got into character by making cute hand gestures and funny facial movements while working on the cartoon series and then over to the adult studio to make obscene hand gestures and contortionist movements while panting and groaning for an hour. I always figured Ted must be bipolar

It's no wonder he was slightly crazy and totally unreliable. But he had a great sense of humour, so I hired him to work for me. Through the course of the next three years, I fired and rehired Ted at least fifty times. He was constantly showing up late and I was constantly giving him one last chance to smarten up. He would listen quietly, promised to be more reliable and punctual in the future and then walk in late the next day. I'd fire him again and the next day he would show up on time and start back to work as if nothing happened. I would have killed him if I didn't like him so much. One day he asked me to hire his brother Stephen. I did and immediately started to question my sanity. I remember buying a beautiful light fixture and asking Stephen to hang it in the window and light it up. Two hours later, Stephen finished this half-hour job and the fixture was looking beautiful. I told him to put an exceptionally high price on the lamp and hoped it would sell quickly. While Marilyn and I were busy stocking our shelves and Stephen was serving behind the counter a man, noticing the fixture in the window, entered the store asking the price. Stephen quoted a price even higher than the exceptionally high one I had given him. The man accepted without question and then Stephen refused to sell it to him. The customer angrily left the store and I stood dumbfounded. I finally came to my senses and rushed to the door to try to save the sale. It was too late. I walked over to Stephen and screamed, "What the hell do you think you're doing? " He said he had spent two hours putting up the fixture in the window and it looked beautiful so he decided he wasn't going to sell it, I reminded him that I was the boss, it was my shop and I was in the business of buying and selling and that the reason the fixture was placed in the window in the first place was to guarantee its sale. He insisted that the fixture was not for sale at any price and no one could change his mind. It was a Salvador Dalí moment. I was in a surrealistic dream. Stephen told me he would quit before he would sell the fixture. I said, "BYE".

Stories of treasures found

We all dream of one day finding that treasure chest filled with precious jewels and knowing that we are suddenly set for the rest of our lives. Books such as "The Count of Monte Cristo" or "Treasure Island" captivate us. We run out to buy lottery tickets or watch quiz shows to share in the thrill of new-found wealth. I've never found that elusive mother lode that would turn my life around but, over the years, I did find some interesting treasures that, if nothing else, brought a smile to my face.

19TH CENTURY CANADIAN MILITARY RESERVE JACKET

I'll never forget the day I found this early 19th century Canadian Military reserve jacket. The house was in the city of Beaconsfield and I had just purchased an assortment of porcelain tableware. While packing the dishes in the plastic container I had brought for the occasion, I noticed that I was

short on wrapping paper. Having just paid two hundred dollars for the tableware, I didn't want it arriving at its final destination in pieces so I asked the lady of the house if she had any wrapping materials. "Will this do?" she asks, pulling out this beautiful old military jacket, "it's been lying around the house for years and I'm tired of looking at it. I was planning on ripping it up and using it for dusters but you can have it to wrap the dishes. I'll get other dusters."

The historic value of the jacket far outweighed its monetary value and its monetary value far outweighted the total value of the dishes I had purchased.

It's unfortunate that a lot of our history ends up in the landfills and scrapyards of this nation. I'm always saddened when people sell off their old family photos and family memorabilia with the attitude "It's all garbage to me."

19TH CENTURY NORTHUMBERLAND FUSILIERS SWORD

This sword dating to the late 1800s was purchased at a garage sale for ten dollars. The entire blade of the sword is acid engraved with the battle honors of the Northumberland Fusiliers.

This prized possession chronicling over a hundred years of military history eventually worked its way into the wrong hands and ended up being tossed carelessly on the ground with other cast-offs.

History must be rescued from the hands of the indifferent.

COLLECTION OF MILITARY MEDALS RETRIEVED FROM THE GARBAGE BIN

After purchasing a number of items from a household, I was on my way out the door when I noticed a picture of a soldier on the wall. "You wouldn't have anything military to sell ?" I asked. "Not really," the lady of the house replied. "I had a box full of old medals but I threw them all in the garbage." Looking shocked I asked, "When did they get tossed out?" "Just before you arrived, I've been doing some spring cleaning today and clearing out all the junk in the house." she said. "Please tell me the garbage truck hasn't passed yet," I pleaded. She informed me that the garbage didn't pass for at least another hour so we went outside and she found the recently disposed-of box at the top of a garbage bag. I opened the box and discovered medals at least five times more valuable than the items she had just sold me in the house. One woman's trash was indeed one man's treasure that time around.

BURROUGHES & WATTS CHAMPIONSHIP POOL CUES

As I arrived at a garage sale in the town of Baie D'Urfe and noticed a man holding two nineteenth century tin containers marked five dollars each. I discreetly watched him as he

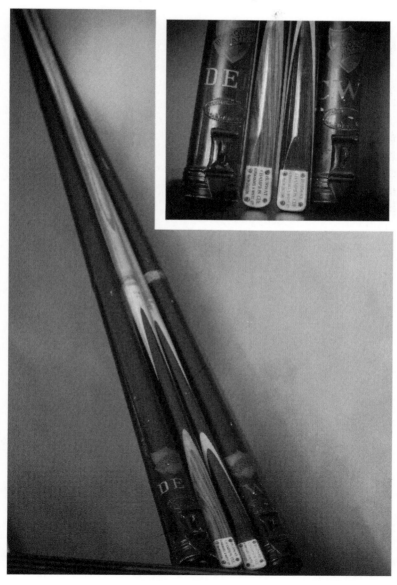

opened one container and pulled out a magnificent pool cue with an ivory inlay handle. "Late again," I thought, "maybe it will be my turn next time." Just as those words were flashing through my mind and to my total amazement, the man rejected the two containers containing the pool cues and placed them back on the property owner's lawn.

I slowly, but not too slowly, picked them up, paid the $10 and walked off with my two Burroughes & Watts, Royal Warrant from her Majesty Queen Victoria, championship pool cues.

God was smiling down upon me that day. I would gladly have paid $200 for the tin containers alone.

QING DYNASTY FIGURINES

These two *famille verte* figurines dating back to the late seventeenth to early eighteenth century or Kangxi period of the Qing Dynasty were found at the bottom of a cardboard box filled with the cast-offs from a Westmount home. The family had gone through the home taking anything they believed to be of any value. They called me in at the last minute to see if I would purchase the junk left behind. I was happy to be of service. Anything I didn't purchase was headed right for the garbage. Maybe archeologists are looking in the wrong place for their artifacts.

Early 18th Century Qing Dynasty figurines

MUSEUM QUALITY WATERCOLOR

This amazing watercolor by Henry Henshall RWS entitled "*The Tragedy*" was purchased as part of a package deal from a home that was being vacated.

I assumed that it was just an interesting print judging from the other discarded items that were included in the package. Throwing the painting in a box loaded with the other items purchased that day, I thought no more about it until I arrived back at the store. Once I had a chance to study it more carefully, I discovered it was indeed an original watercolor and one of the best I had seen to date.

Because watercolors are usually created on paper and framed behind glass they are constantly being mistaken as prints by sellers and greatly undersold.

Art is in the eye of the beholder and what one man or woman feels is offensive, ugly, unprofessional, or simply lacking in talent another might consider a masterpiece. I make a point of investigating any serious work of art that comes my way before setting a price.

I check out *findartinfo.com*, *artnet*, and other auction value sites on the computer and also refer to Benezit Dictionary of Artists and other published books on art auction values sometimes found in libraries.

I am very careful about purchasing paintings. There are lots of wonderful painted reproductions being made today and many art students and forgers can duplicate the masters.

After purchasing a beautiful Cornelius Krieghoff copy from a master Canadian forger I asked him to sign his name to the painting because I admired his talent if not his occupation. Over tea, he showed me auction catalogue after auction catalogue describing his works as attributed to great artists or listed as coming from the Dutch school. He found the latter description amusing because the only reason for that designation was the fact that he happened to be of Dutch descent. He told me how he would search all the flea markets and second hand shops looking for original antique frames, and canvases to paint over. If he couldn't find an old canvas in time to supply his customer he would just add his own special solution onto the newer canvas.

When I questioned him on how he was able to stay one step ahead of the law, he told me he never put a false signature on a canvas and the auction galleries he dealt with all knew they were dealing with copies. They protected themselves by describing his painting as, *attributed* to, or *from the Dutch school*, in all their catalogues.

SMITH & WESSON TIP-UP REVOLVERS

These two beauties were picked up at a garage sale about 12 years ago for the grand sum of $300. That was a hunk of change compared to what I usually had to pay out at garage sales and my wife was not pleased with the purchase.

She calmed down a bit when I told her they were antique from the 1860s and that ammunition was no longer available.

These Smith & Wesson Tip-up revolvers were the same make and model as a gun sold at auction that was allegedly used in Canada's first Political Assassination in 1868, that of Thomas D'Arcy McGee. That gun sold for over one hundred thousand dollars.

What a difference a little political history and solid providence can make on the end value of an item.

SELF-PUBLISHED NOTMAN BOOKS

Recovered from the garbage by an observant neighbor in Montreal, these three volumes of self-published photographs by the famous Montreal photographer William Notman are titled Portraits of British Americans.

Notman was the first Canadian to be recognized internationally for his photographic skills. The fact that these three volumes, which have a historical as well as a monetary value, were minutes away from being crushed in a garbage disposal truck is disconcerting. We should thank God sometimes for nosy neighbours.

ANCIENT ROMAN GLASS

This piece of ancient Roman glass was discarded among many other items by a woman vacating an old mansion she could no longer afford to live in. The taxes on the mansion were higher than the price she and her husband had initially paid for the property many, many decades ago when they were reasonably well off.

The municipal government now believed it had the right to take this woman's home away for back taxes. The fact that it wasn't a mansion to this elderly lady but only a home with a

lot of personal history in which she eventually wished to die, meant nothing to the bureaucrats.

The small glass container from ancient Rome had only a value of approximately two to three hundred dollars, but then again it was not subjected to yearly re-evaluations over the centuries and the heavy tax increases that would eventually destroy it.

EARLY VICTORIAN STERLING CANDLESTICKS

While working in my shop one day a lady came in with a cardboard box filled with old, discolored silverware. She

dropped the rather heavy box on my counter stating that she was in a bit of a hurry so could I quickly look at the silver plated items in the box and offer her a reasonable price. I told her that I would be with her in a minute to which she replied," "Listen, just give me twenty-five dollars and take the box, whatever you don't want, throw out."

After taking a quick look at the top items, I figured the deal looked reasonable so I paid the twenty-five dollars, placed the box on the floor and went back to my other work.

Approximately fifteen minutes later, an antique dealer I recognized came into the store, noticed the box and asked if he could look through it. "Go ahead" I said, "It's just a bunch of old silver plated pieces badly in need of a polishing."

Digging deeply into the box he pulls out two silver candlesticks, studies them closely and then asks the price. "I didn't even know they were in there," I declared, "Give me a minute and I'll get around to pricing them." "I'll give you $100 for them," he said and the early bullshit warning system immediately went off in my head. "Let me take a fast look first," I said picking up the candlesticks. Looking closely, I noticed a very small early Victorian sterling silver hallmark on both candlesticks dating them back to the first half of the 19th century and giving them a very healthy value. I had gotten lucky and this dealer was ready and eager to take that luck away. "If you add another nineteen hundred to that offer, I might accept," I said and watched as he walked out of the store dejectedly.

17TH CENTURY ENGLISH OAK COFFER

This 17th century English Oak coffer was found at a house sale in a middle to low-income area in Montreal.

Along with this chest, I purchased an 18th century lowboy that was in extremely bad condition. I remember bringing it into the basement area of my store and asking my handyman Tom what he thought of it. "It will make great firewood," he said, "I hope you didn't actually pay out good money for it."

Approximately a week later, I brought an American dealer down into the basement and while Tom looked on, I negotiated a price of one thousand dollars for the busted up lowboy.

I helped the dealer bring the piece to his van and then I returned to the basement to revive Tom.

Treasures can and are found everywhere so it is sometimes foolish to disregard a call from a client just because she or he lives in a poorer class neighborhood.

THE SWEATERS

It was about two weeks before Christmas and I got a call from
a man claiming to be a customs agent at the airport. He
requested that I meet him in the storage depot near the airport
to discuss some business. When I arrived, Peter, the customs
agent, brought me over to a pallet of packages containing wool
sweaters which had never been claimed. "Since we are neither
a long-term storage depot or a retail shop, we have no use for
them," he said. "Would you be interested in purchasing the
pallet at $4 a sweater?" Since it was just before Christmas and
everybody gives sweaters at Christmas time I accepted his offer,
made out a check, and loaded up what turned out to be
Marilyn's and everybody else's in the neighberhood's Christmas
present.

The sweaters were made from pure one hundred percent wool
and had beautiful winter scenes knitted on them. We only put
out twenty at a time at a selling price of $10 each and they flew
off our shelves. Customers would buy 5 to 10 sweaters and
sometimes come back for more. Everybody was in a great
mood until the day after Christmas when they started to walk
around town and noticed everybody else wearing the same
sweater.

THE RUG

While working in my first shop. I befriended two young men
who did odd jobs for the landlord. He called the boys if he
needed walls to be plastered, an apartment painted or an area
cleaned at any of his many buildings. They were reliable,
honest, good at their jobs and worked cheap. They also knew
nothing about antiques. Fancy things at fancy prices meant
little to them because extravagant embellishments didn't quite
fit into the hard world they lived in. While doing a clean up or
preparing a vacant apartment for the next tenant, they

sometimes discovered small treasures which they would bring to my store. Some of the treasures ended up being trash, but not always. When they hit something halfway good, the boys would then take the cash and head out for a good meal, washed down with a few cold beers.

One night at about 5 o'clock, I decided to close up shop and bring out the garbage. Arriving at the garbage area, I noticed an interesting carpet thrown among the many discarded bags. Adding my refuse with the rest, I picked up the carpet and dumped it in the front door of the store. A warm fire, a hot supper and a nice chilled glass of wine were waiting for me at home, so I decided to wait and check the rug out in the morning.

That night at about 9 p.m. I receive a panicky telephone call from one of the two boys. After calming him down, I finally got the story out. The landlord told them to clean out the basement of one of his upscale appartment buildings. Because garbage pick-up in that area wasn't for a few more days, they decided to dump the garbage they collected at the building where the store was located. The rug was included with the garbage and that was the reason for the call. It seems a woman in one of the high-class apartments was having a party that Saturday night and she didn't want any wine stains on her twenty thousand dollar antique silk Persian rug so she had it bundled up and left in the dry secure basement area for the evening. The boys found it, figured it was garbage and hauled it off with the rest of the trash. By the time they arrived back at the apartment building, the tenant had noticed her missing rug, called the landlord and was threatening legal action against everyone concerned. She was throwing a serious temper tantrum. The landlord, surmising what must have happened, ordered the boys to return the rug immediately or face firing and possible arrest.

Rushing back to the garbage heap, they discovered everything had been picked up. In one last act of desperation, they decided to check out my store in the vain hope that I had noticed the rug in the garbage and salvaged it. Praise the Lord. It was their lucky day. There it was bundled up on the floor just beside my glass door. That's when I received the call. Having some fun at their expense, I told the boys that the rug was legally mine. Finders-keepers was the way I rationalized it. After listening to their pleading for a few minutes, my hard shell broke and I told them to relax and notify the lady that the rug could be picked up in the morning.

The next call I received was from the woman insisting that I bring the rug to her home immediately or else. That got my Irish up. Who the hell did she think she was? "Or else what?" I said, "if it wasn't for your criminal stupity the rug would be on your floor right now. It's not the boys fault, it's yours. The only reason your rug isn't an elegant home for the junkyard rats right now is because of my intervention."

She was further informed that the only reason I was returning the rug was to save the boys some aggravation and the loss of their jobs. "You will personally come to my store tomorrow to pick it up (OR ELSE) it will end up in the trash where I found it." I assured her.

The next morning she arrived, picked up the twenty thousand dollar rug and left without a thank you.

THE COMIC BOOKS

Who would ever think that a comic book that sold for ten cents in June of 1938 would sell at auction for one million dollars in 2010? The price might not have gone up faster than a speeding bullet but it definitely took flight. Check the auction records for the last twenty years, and you will find amazing paintings by famous artists selling for a considerably lower price than this old Action #1 Superman comic book. Hopefully, this isn't an accurate reflection of our North American capitalist mentality.

The reality of it is that there are big kids and investers out there with unlimited resources who are ready to pay high prices for some old comic books. A small fortune in early comic books came into my hands and I blew it.

An elderly lady brought me into a large dry basement in her home in the west end of the city to show me a number of items she had for sale. Out of the corner of my eye, I noticed a large dome top trunk from the 1880s I made a mental note to ask her about it before leaving but unfortunately I was in a bit of a hurry that day and left the house forgetting all about the trunk. Two weeks later, we had heavy rainfall causing massive flooding throughout the west end. Thankfully, my store was spared the disaster so it was business as usual when I received a call from the same lady. Once more she brought me down to her basement where she had items displayed for my consideration. I noted the dampness of the basement and asked if she had been hit hard by the flooding. "Yes," she said, "the basement got flooded but thank God, there was nothing of any real value down here." I completed our business and, on the way out, remembered to ask about the large dome trunk in the corner. She told me that it was for sale but unfortunately got damaged in the flood. She had meant to discuss the trunk and its contents with me last time but could see I was in a bit of a hurry so she decided to leave it for another day. "What contents?" I asked and she then informed me it contained her brother's comic collection. I walked over, opened the trunk and discovered it was filled to the brim with old ten cent comics. There were Action comics, Marvel comics, Detective comics, Wizz comics, there was Superman, Captain America, Batman and Flash comics and every one was totally destroyed by water.

They were matted together in one big bulk of comic hell. The trunk must have been totally submerged. Leaving the basement, I felt like I could qualify as a new comic book character.

STUPIDMAN
DENSER THAN A CEMENT BLOCK
MORE SORROWFUL THAN A FUNERAL PROCESSION
WANTING TO LEAP TALL BUILDINGS
IN A SINGLE BOUND.

FIRST SUPERMAN COMIC SELLS FOR 3.2 MILLION DOLLARS

IF ONLY HE KNEW...!

The criminal element

Marilyn and I have had our share of excitement over the years. A store dealing in second-hand goods attracts its share of shady characters and they are not always easy to recognize. If they all came in with black leather jackets and sweat shirts proclaiming

HAPPINESS IS A WARM GUN

it would be great. Unfortunately, that isn't the case. Some dress in three piece suits and look like politicians, some *are* politicians.

A man wearing a three-piece suit came into my store wanting to know if I was interested in purchasing a Persian rug. His story was that his company went bankrupt and he was selling household goods to get by. The rug was out in his car. I went to check it over and purchased it for a thousand dollars. Two well-dressed gentlemen come into my shop a few days later asking if I had recently purchased a Persian rug. Having bought the rug in good faith I said "Yes it's in my back office." Their brother, they informed me, had a drinking and drug problem and had gone to his mother's home and lifted the rug off the dining room floor. The mother was away on holiday and didn't know about the theft. The plan was to retrieve the rug, replace it before she came home from holidays and then get their brother into a rehab center. The description of the brother matched that of the seller. I brought them into the office and showed them the rug in question. It, of course, was the mother's. Police involvement was not an option, they said, because that would only further upset their fragile mother so they returned the purchase price, picked up the rug and left.

When dealing in second-hand goods, these situations are bound to happen no matter how careful you are.

A respectable-looking young man in casual clothes came into my store with a case full of camera equipment for sale. While checking out the equipment, I asked the price. "A friend gave me the equipment in payment for an outstanding debt," he said, "all I want is the initial amount of the loan back." At that time, I didn't know much about camera equipment but at the price of two hundred dollars, I knew I couldn't go wrong. Before purchasing it I told him I needed two pieces of idenfication, information regarding his name, date of birth, height, weight, address, and telephone number for the police report I was required to fill out when purchasing used equipment. He was made very aware of the importance of verifying that the equipment was not stolen because the police would shortly be receiving my report and if proven stolen, he would be arrested. "My friend is an honest man," he said. "There will be no problem." I bought the equipment and submitted my report. A week later two detectives showed up at my store to recover the stolen camera equipment that had been taken from a local university. They gave me a receipt and took the equipment with them. A month later I received a summons to appear in court.

I expected a call from the young man's defense attorney requesting my version of the incident but it never came. His plan, I discovered, was to put me on the stand and portray me as a shady character who couldn't be trusted. Unfortuately, he decided to break a basic courtroom rule—

NEVER ASK A QUESTION
UNLESS YOU ALREADY KNOW THE ANSWER

I got up on the stand giving my name and general information and the prosecution attorney asked me two simple questions:

Did I buy the camera equipment?

Who did I buy it from?

I answered truthfully and it was the defense attorney's turn.

"Mr Hicks, did you pay $200 for the camera equipment specified?"

"Yes sir, I did."

"You know that the equipment you claim you purchased from my client is worth $3,000."

"I know that now, I didn't at the time. I have little knowledge of photographic equipment. I just knew a bargain when I saw one."

"I'm sure you do, Mr. Hicks. I'm sure you do"

"Yes sir, I do."

"Mr. Hicks, have you ever been in trouble with the law?" (That's where he made the big mistake that cost his client his freedom.)

"No sir, I've never been in trouble with the law, not as a child, not as a teenager, and definitely not as an adult."

"You do know the penalty for perjury, Mr. Hicks?"

"No sir, I do not and I don't much care because I never plan to give perjured testimony."

"That will be all."

"But I want to say something."

"Thank you, Mr. Hicks that will be all!"

The Judge then said,' Thank you, Mr. Hicks, you're excused."

I found out later that the young man had a past criminal record so he was found guilty and sentenced to jail time. I believed then, as I believe now, that he was innocent.

If only the defense attorney had taken the time to talk to me before the trial and ask the right questions.

Did my client supply you with his true name, address, and phone number?

Yes.

Did you explan to my client that a report with this information was going to the police?

Yes.

Did my client supply you with proper picture ID?

Yes.

Did my client tell you that the equipment was given to him by a friend in payment for a loan?

Yes.

Did you warn the seller that he would be arrested if the equipment was stolen?

Yes.

In your opinion, did the seller know he was selling stolen merchandise?

No.

Final verdict NOT GUILTY.

That was the way it should have gone.

This is one case where the client should have been set free and the lawyer should have been thrown in jail for incompetence.

These two examples pale in comparison with an unfortunate incident that happened to a Notre Dame Street dealer. He received a call from a home in an affluent section of town. The caller said his mother was in a long-term medical facility and would not be returning home. Her apartment had to be cleared because the lease was almost up. The nearest family members lived far away and had enough of their own belongings to contend with. The dealer naturally rushed to the appointment and was met at the door by a distinguished man looking quite relaxed and comfortable. He told the dealer that he was a very busy out-of-town businessman, and didn't have a lot of time to spend looking around for the best deal. "I will sell everything to the first dealer who makes me a fair offer," he stated. The man then made himself a coffee in the kitchen while the dealer explored the apartment.

Both men then sat down at the kitchen table, exchanged pleasantries over coffee and got down to business. An amount was agreed upon and a time set for pick up. The following day the dealer showed up at the location with a moving truck, met the client, paid the agreed upon amount in cash as requested and started to load up. The seller excused himself, saying that the experience was just too painful. He told the dealer that it was a secure apartment complex so he should just close the door after he had finished.

The following day a convoy of police cars show up at the Notre Dame Street shop. After scaring the dealer half to death the truth finally came out. The apartment the dealer cleaned out belonged to a couple that were away on holiday. The man in the apartment had neutralized the alarm system, picked the lock and made himself at home. Since the couple occupying the apartment had just recently moved in, no one questioned his presence. The moving van, however, was another matter. One of the tenants, suspicious of why a resident would suddenly be moving out after just moving in, copied down the license number of the moving truck and called the police. Police were slow to react and arrived after the van had departed but solid police follow-up work led to the recovery of the stolen goods and the heart condition of the antique dealer (it's amazing how your stress level increases on seeing five police cars pulling up outside your place of business).

Shoplifters

Shoplifters, I discovered, are very difficult to profile. They come in different shapes, age groups, sexes, occupations, and nationalities. Some are easy to spot by their ever shifting eyes, nervous movements and attempts to hide from sight. The professsionals are more relaxed, confident, sometimes charming and often well-equiped. They often try to put you off your guard by being friendly, helpful and inquisitive. They distract you while their partner helps himself, or herself, to your best pieces. Knowing this, I still can't help but be annoyed when I walk into a store and find a store detective dogging my every movement. You know you're not there to steal but the point is, he doesn't. Maybe he should do it with a little more discretion, but he has a job to do and it is an important job. It was estimated that shoplifters cost retailers approximately twenty-five million dollars a day in the United States. When you're a small business a good shoplifter can wipe out your profits for the day, week and even a month. I seldom prosecute shoplifters because it takes up a lot of my time to little avail. A pregnant woman came into my store and stole a Royal Doulton figurine. I waited till she left the shop and approached her asking for the figurine back. She, of course, denied any wrongdoing so I offered her a choice.

"You can either remove the figurine from its hiding place, return it to me and go on your way, never to return to my store again, or we can wait for the police to arrive. The decision is yours," I told her. After a slight pause she removed the figurine from her coat and returned it to me. "Thank you for doing the right and smart thing," I said, "I hope that child of yours grows up to have a mother to be proud of." I had no idea what was going on in her life, all I knew was that humiliating her in front of a judge and spectators would accomplish nothing.

It's hard not to develop a degree of paranoia in this business.

Some people believe there is a degree of larceny in all of us and the difference between a criminal and a law-abiding citizen is just a matter of degrees. Maybe that's true, but then again maybe it isn't, I prefer to believe the latter.

Approximately twenty-five years ago when I had a little more religion in my heart I wrote a song called, "The Reason The Why" with the chorus:

Why children do suffer
Why mothers know grief
Why all men must toil
Why the saint, why the thief

My Jesus, I love you
I know when I die
You'll have all the answers
The reason's the why

There have been a few incidents that have shaken my faith in the integrity of people. An older lady named Grace would frequent my store and buy a few items from time to time. She was always friendly, helpful and brought in home cooking on a few occasions. Marilyn and I developed a real affection for her.

One day a friend of mine was visiting my store and noticed Grace. Steve, the proud owner of a popular book store, called me aside and told me that Grace had been in his store buying a book when a number of books fell out from inside her heavy overcoat as she stood at the cash. She apologized for her indiscretion, paid for all the books and left the store.

After hearing the story, Marilyn and I made it a point to watch her a little more carefully from then on. A week later she entered the store with a large bag under her arm, looked around and then walked out after commenting on what a beautiful day it was. Marilyn immediately informed me that she had hidden a leather briefcase behind the bag she was carrying and walked out with it. I approached Grace outside the shop and asked her if she had forgotten something. She said no, and I suggested that she take a look behind her shopping bag. "Oh, I'm so sorry," she said, "I forgot I picked that up."

"Please be a little more careful in the future" I stated as I took back the brief case and returned to the store.

Another wealthy customer of mine would steal jewelry. Her little trick was to try on a number of pieces pocketing one of them when I lost count or my attention was drawn away. She would constantly chatter about her life in order to distract me from her true purpose. It was after losing a Cartier watch to this lady that I finally clued in to her. The next time she came in, I told her to keep her hands out of the jewelry case and that she would henceforth be shown only one piece at a time. She got the hint.

I remember telling Marilyn never to let anyone put their hands in the jewelry case because of the possibility of theft. "Don't worry, I'm very observent," she said "It's hard to steal with me watching." "Not that hard," I replied. To prove the point, I told a friend of mine, an amateur magician, to steal jewelry while my wife watched.

She opened the jewelry case and let Tony handle a few pieces while her focus was totally fixed on his hands. After about two minutes, she closed the case again, "So did he get anything?" I asked. "Not a thing," she replied confidently. I told Tony to hand over the stolen jewelry and, to her astonishment, he dropped three gold rings into her hand.

I have never lost faith in the honest nature of most people and I often think back to the day when a child returned to my store after making a small purchase for his mother and handed me a ten dollar bill saying," Mister, you gave me too much change."

I said, "Thanks Kid, it's been a tough day but you just made it so much better, keep it"

It was the best ten dollars I have ever spent.

Break ins

I guess I should consider myself lucky. In twenty eight years of business I've only had three break-ins and was instrumental in catching the bad guys and recovering the loot in one of them.

My first time, so to speak, was at approximately 3a.m. on a Saturday night. There's nothing like the adrenaline rush you experience when you awaken in the middle of the night to the sound of your telephone ringing. The first thought is that someone is hurt, in trouble or dead. When it turns out to be a wrong number or a crank call, you wish the caller was hurt, in trouble or dead. The call that night was to inform me that my store alarm had just gone off. I quickly dressed and rushed to the store hoping for the best but suspecting the worst. On arrival, I discovered someone had smashed the glass front door of my store and grabbed the ten-speed bike that was parked just inside the doorway. The bike wasn't valuable so the police and I came to the conclusion that someone too drunk to drive came from the bar across the street and decided to peddle rather than walk home. He was sober enough to know he couldn't drive, just not sober enough to realize that break and entering was also a serious crime. They say every cloud has a silver lining. No one was killed by that particular drunk driver that night. Maybe my cheap bike saved a life.

I discovered the second robbery when I arrived at the store one morning and noticed a hole cut into the bottom of my back door and about 300 records, along with other miscellaneous items missing. The rats must have scurried in through the hole, collected their loot and scurried back out. The police arrived approximately forty-five minutes after being called (there must have been a two for one sale at Dunkin' Donuts), took down a report of what happened and left. In my naivety, I expected the full CSI (Crime Scene Investigation) treatment so I was greatly disappointed. It was obvious by their attitude that there was not going to be a follow-up investigation even after I informed them that I strongly suspected the three young men had recently moved upstairs from the store. This real world was so much different from the popular world of entertainment I had come to know and love.

I decided to take the law into my own hands and call every major second-hand record store in the city. I hit pay dirt on call number three, "Your three packages are waiting here for you now, sir." the store manager said after I finished explaining what had happened. At first I was slightly confused by his reply but suddenly caught on and said," Do they have approximately three hundred records with them and do the records have small red and white labels bearing a hand written price?"

"That's correct sir," he answered. After asking him to delay purchasing the records for as long as possible, I hung up and called the police. The three boys that I had initially suspected were caught with their hands in the cookie jar and immediately arrested. The Pink Panther strikes again.

My last break-in occurred when I stupidly left a beautiful sword on display in my front window. Once more I was awakened in the middle of the night to rush to my store and discovered a broken window and missing sword.

That was the last time I ever made that mistake.

Tweedle Dee and Tweedle Dumb

Dee and Dumb were two plain-clothes police officers that would come into my store weekly to collect the reports on items purchased and to browse around looking for stolen merchandise. They must have shopped at "Cops R Us" because they always came in looking like the Pink Panther's Inspector Clouseau. Dee considered himself somewhat of a ladies' man and was always trying to hit upon Marilyn. Since Marilyn had a perfectly good set of eyes and a nose that could smell bullshit a mile away, his feeble attempts to impress her went nowhere. Dumb was anything but a ladies' man. His girlfriend, I later discovered, had already shot him once and on another occasion attempted to stab him. He had the face of a crucified crumpet, and the personality to match. In the approximately ten years they came into my store, they never once found anything stolen but that didn't stop them from trying. Once they gave me a citation after I had purchased a broken down TV from the home of an elderly man that needed a few dollars to get by the rest of the week. My act of kindness ended up costing me $300 for failing to complete the required paper work for the purchase. In another instance, they came into my store to collect a report on some electronic equipment I had purchased. I noticed Dumb eyeing the equipment in an acquisitive manner. Turning to Marilyn, I said "I'll give you twenty to one odds they come back falsely claiming that the equipment is stolen property." Two days later, I won my bet but lost my equipment when Dee and Dumb came walking into the store to confiscate the alleged stolen property. They took the items away without leaving a receipt as required by police policy. I never heard another word about the incident.

Not all thieves wear masks. Some wear uniforms.

* My son's a police officer so I have a great deal of respect for the many good police officiers out there, it's the ones who abuse the power we give them that I sincerely hope end up spending their days praying for soap on a rope to make their prison stay more tolerable.

Store number two

My business started to expand and I was running out of space so when the apartment next door to the store became available I took over the lease and had all the walls taken down. My shop was now twice its original size and that was still not enough space. A second store became available within half a block of store number one. It was in the basement of an apartment building next door to a funeral home so I was able to negotiate a pretty good lease. The new landlord was a tall overweight Greek professional cook that always looked penniless and on his last legs. He loved antiques and I honestly believe he bought almost as much as he pocketed.

The funeral home wasn't exactly ecstatic about having a second hand store next door. It's tough having a funeral with a pick- up truck full of old second-hand furniture parked next to the hearse. People would start to wonder, "Maybe you *can* take it with you." When I knew there was going to be a funeral I would always park a block away but that still didn't endear me to the manager of the funeral home. I think I pissed him off when I suggested that I was planning to open my own Irish crematorium and call it, "Wake and Bake." The man had no sense of humor which wasn't surprising considering some of his deceased customers looked in better shape than he was.

Coming in and going out, my business was expanding and I was riding the wave. An old customer named Mary was hired to operate store number two. She was a single mother with one child surviving on welfare so the small salary helped keep her and her son just over the poverty line. Her husband was in jail on a manslaughter charge. She was worried that he would one day be released and go back to using her as his personal punching bag. Business was going good at my first store but didn't really pick up in the second store until I replaced Mary with someone with more sales experience. I like to believe that was the only reason for the sudden increase in sales. It's a big job trying to keep two stores going when you're the only buyer and it was even tougher when store number three came along.

My loving and crazy wife

People say familiarity breeds contempt. That might be the case with some people but it definitely isn't the case with Marilyn and me. We have worked side by side for 30 years and we haven't once come close to killing each other. This hundred twenty pound, five foot six dynamo has worked long hours and helped carry sofas, bureaus and armoires up and down stairways without once complaining. To tell the truth she might have complained once or twice, maybe three or four, possibly even five or six times. But who's counting?

Men looked upon her in wonder as they watched her unload my truck. Some gentlemen would offer to help just to be told, "That's alright, I can handle it."

I love Marilyn dearly but sometimes she drives me absolutely crazy. One summer I had just unloaded a bunch of merchandise and started to head out on the road again leaving her to watch the store. Among the items I had purchased that day was an old 22 rifle that I placed behind the counter for safekeeping. Before putting it there, I checked to verify that the gun was empty and there was no bullet in the chamber. While I was away three teenaged punks came into my store looking for trouble. They were loud, vulgar, and annoying. One of them went to the counter Marilyn was standing behind and intentionally knocked over a display. She told him to be more careful and to pick the display up. His reaction was, "Fuck you, I'm not picking anything up, what you going to do about it, bitch." He then called out to his friends and started around the counter. Marilyn, without blinking, picked up the unloaded rifle, stuck it under his chin and said, "I'm going to blow your fucking head off." The punk yelled out, "Let's get the hell out of here. This bitch is crazy." They ran out of the store never to return. That time she could have gotten herself killed. Once she almost got me killed.

Marilyn is an animal lover and goes ballistic if she sees any animal being mistreated. One freezing cold day I arrived at my store to find Marilyn in an aggravated state. Knowing of her love for animals, the flower store owner next door came in to tell her about a dog tied to a post outside the bar across the street. He said the dog had been there in the freezing temperature without shelter for over an hour while the owner was inside drinking. My wife then asked me to watch the store while she went over and kicked the dog owner's ass. I didn't need a lawsuit and I definitely didn't want to see Marilyn hurt so I said I would take charge of the situation. I should state here that I have very poor eyesight, and without my glasses, I am virtually blind.

Entering the bar, I politely asked who owned the dog outside. A gruff looking man seated on a bar stool said, "It's mine, what's it to you? " I told him that while he sat nice and cozy in the bar, his dog was freezing outside with no way of keeping warm. I suggested he take the dog home and then return to his drinking alone. His response to my request was a simple, "Fuck off." At that point I lost my cool and invited him outside to settle the matter. To show this miserable excuse for a human being that I meant business, as I walked to the glass front door I took off my glasses and put on my best tough guy look. Taking off my glasses was a mistake. I realized that when I collided head first into the glass front door of the bar almost knocking myself out. When we both got outside, my opponent turned his back to me, untied his dog and left for home. I honestly believe that I scared the hell out of him that day and it was just a nervous laugh I heard as he walked away.

I love Marilyn dearly. She has the unique ability to make me laugh no matter how badly I might be feeling at the time and what that woman does to the English language would make any French nationalist stand up and cheer. "Whistle while you work" that beloved song from the Disney children's classic "Snow White and The Seven Dwarfs" became "Whistle while you jerk" when Marilyn innocently sang it. That conjured up image of the dwarfs still invades my mind. After viewing, "The Sound of Music", we decided to go on a walk and as we walked, Marilyn started to sing "A Few of My Favorite Things" only the lyrics came out, "When the dog bites, when the bee humps, when I'm feeling low." I had to point out to Marilyn that the bee was stinging, not humping.

Anyone not knowing Marilyn would believe she was intentionally making those changes but I can assure you they are totally unintentional and totally innocent. A few more Marilynisms, as I refer to them, are the new names she assigned to birds that came into the bird shelter she works at part time, the Purple Martin became the Paul Martin (ex-prime minister of Canada). Yellow Warbler became the yellow wallaby, much to the amusement of our New Zealand friend and the Scoter duck became the Scrotum duck.

I will never forget the day she came home and told me she was worried about her little scrotum because it wasn't eating. There were so many Marilynisms that I can't possibly list them all or, for that fact, remember them all because they have become so commonplace that they often go unnoticed. One I did take note of, however, was when she informed me that her bird rehabilitating friend Lynn was having trouble completing her feces for her doctorate degree. I told her it might have something to do with Lynn's diet and she looked at me like I was crazy.

Marilyn is a beautiful, bright and loving woman and her unique treatment of the English language is one of the many things I dearly love about her.

House calls

House calls can be very interesting and at the same time very scary. You never know what to expect when walking into the home of a stranger, especially when that stranger knows you have a pocket full of money. Just as they are strangers to you, you're a stranger to them so cheque books are often useless on these calls.

A Laurentian antique dealer was murdered after being lured to a country home with a promise of a house full of Victorian furniture. Another one I knew personally was robbed and then murdered in his home situated above his antique store - part of the dangers of the trade.

Some of our calls are amusing like the time I got a request to go to an older woman's home to purchase some jewelry. She was in her late eighties and although her body was aging, her mind was still fresh and young. She brought me into her bedroom to inspect the jewelry and I made my selection. We settled on a price and as I was paying her, she looked up at me with a twinlkle in her eye and said, "Son, you've no idea how long it's been since a man gave me money in my bedroom."

In another instance, I got a call from an older woman asking me to call in at her house and check out a daybed and antique chair she had for sale. I recognized her voice as belonging to a customer that regularily came into my store to buy small items. She seemed lonely so I would always take the time to talk to her. Arriving at her home, I rang the bell and she answered the door wearing a totally transparent negligée and a smile. Not knowing how to react, I just acted as if naked women always answered the door to me. I asked her what she had to show me, in retrospect, not the best choice of words, and she brought me into the living room where the daybed and antique chair were located. I purchased them and loaded them into my truck and wished her a good day. She called me back a few more times after that but, thereafter, always answered the door fully dressed.

There were scary moments too. A widowed woman called me to her home to purchase some of her husband's old equipment. Before his death from a heart attack, he worked as a private investigator. She had all kinds of sophisticated surveillance equipment and a Browning 45 automatic pistol for sale. I asked to see the gun so she brought me down to the basement, opened her safe and removed the gun. She removed it with her finger on the trigger, and the muzzle pointed at my stomach. I gently took the 45 from her hand to check if it was loaded.

The safety was off, the trigger was cocked, the magazine was loaded and there was a bullet in the chamber. It also had a sensitive trigger. The slightest pressure on her finger would have discharged the gun and made a rather large hole in my stomach. Her husband stored it that way because he wanted to be sure that in any home invasion, he would get the bad guy before the bad guy got him. When they made him open his safe, it would be the last thing they ever did.

That was frightening but it was a minor fright compared to what I experienced a short time later in an apartment on Cote des Neiges while looking through some record albums a family was selling. Seated on the couch I flipped through the albums when, suddenly, behind one of the albums, about fifty cockroaches came scurrying out. I jumped up, told the family I had no interest in anything from their house and hurried home to take a bath.

I had nightmares for weeks after that.

73

Many of my calls were uneventful but a few will always stick in my mind. The home in a nice neighboorhood in Montreal West with wall-to-wall dog shit and girls injecting drugs in every room of the house or the home in Pointe Claire where a trustee showed me around explaining that the owner of the property killed his wife in an act of jealousy and then killed himself while two young children lay asleep in their bedroom. The children survived but were left emotionally scarred for life. For some reason, nothing appealed to me from that home.

There was the beautiful home in Westmount owned by a prominent psychologist who spent many years in China. That house was a treasure trove of old memorabilia and artifacts, from racoon skin coats and flapper dresses from the 1920s, top hats and long flowing robes from the 1800s, gold-handled canes, amazing books, china and early firearms. The strangest items I found while searching through that home was a human skull on a bookshelf and a child's wooden coffin from the early 1800s stored under the stairway in the basement. Leaning against the wall, it looked like something you would see in an old Clint Eastwood western.

You just never know what you will find while searching through a stranger's belongings.

It's a gay life

I'll never forget the cold rainy day I went on a late night call to an apartment in downtown Montreal. I knocked on a door which was immediately opened by the most flamboyantly gay man I have ever met. Dressed in a flowery silk-clinging bathrobe with matching slippers, he welcomed me with a warm smile and kiss on both cheeks. He was effervescent, zany, totally off the wall and an outrageous flirt. I was as uncomfortable as a one-legged man at an ass kicking contest. I just wanted to get our business over as quickly as possible and head out for home. He started to show me a variety of china objects and elaborated on the beauty, uniqueness and quality of each piece. After much bickering, we finally agreed on a price. I paid him, packed the items in a box, tucked my umbrella under my arm and headed for the door. In my haste to depart, I forgot that my umbrella handle was protruding out behind me. The client's double-handled umbrella stand sitting by the door was no match for my protruding umbrella handle and hasty departure. I hooked it and pulled it down smashing it into a hundred pieces. He screeched and I just about passed out..Mary Poppins suddenly transformed into Godzilla. "Oh no, Paul bought me that for our anniversary," he said, "how could you be so clumsy?" I told him I was sorry and he would have other anniversaries. That didn't work, he just got more upset. "It was an accident," I said "I will gladly get you a replacement." "How?" he screamed, "Paul brought me that all the way from China." "I could have saved him the trip," I said, "they're selling them in Chinatown for $49.99." He then turned a beautiful shade of purple, which was definitely his color. I threw $100 on the table, told him to run out and buy two in case of another accident and got the hell out of the house as quickly as possible.

I was always putting my foot in my mouth when it came to dealing with my gay clients. Not long after the incident with the umbrella stand, I was tending store while my Marilyn was off on an errand when a regular came in and started talking about the gay pride parade that was going on in town. She asked my opinion of the parade. What I should have said was, "I'm all for the gay pride parade because it installs a feeling of acceptance and community in men and women that have experienced their share of prejudice and injustice." I should have stated that the men in chaps with exposed asses and the over-the-top transvestites no more represented the gay community than drunks walking down St.Catherine Street with top hats garnished in shamrocks represented the Irish community. That's what I should have said, but that quirky sense of humour of mine had to kick in once more and get me in trouble.

Being heterosexual, I told her, I didn't see the point in it. Heterosexuals didn't have parades every year with heterosexuals walking down St. Catherine Street bumping and grinding their pelvic regions together and flaunting their heterosexuality. "The parade," the way I see it "has more to do with sexual practices than sexual preferences. If we go by that standard, why not have a dildo parade for those fond of battery operated devices, or a masturbation marathon with everyone running separately with their hands in their pockets, or how about a bestiality bash with everyone marching their favorite farm animal downtown." She obviously didn't appreciate my unique sense of humor because my comments went over like a fart in a church pew at high mass. Saying good-bye, she headed out the door as if the store was on fire. Marilyn walked in just as she stormed by. Looking at me, she said, "What did you do now?" I related to her what had transpired and she informed me that the client was a lesbian.

I never saw the lady again.

Over the years I had many gay customers and some of them became good friends. Marilyn and I attended parties, anniversaries, a wedding, and, unfortunately, the funerals of some of them. These days, much to my mother's dismay, the only way to get me into church is for a marriage or a funeral.

I sincerely hope that from now on, I'm only attending marriages.

Store number three

I was busy running around trying to run two shops and keep them supplied when the landlord of my first store, Saul, approached me with a proposition. He had a store that he was unable to rent and wanted to know if I would start up an antique business with him. Over coffee, we agreed that he would supply the store and his wife would be the sales person. In return, I would supply the necessary start-up stock and the know-how and buying power to keep the business running. Any and all purchases that were the result of calls coming in to store number three would remain in store number three. All profits that were not put back into inventory were to be divided evenly. We closed the deal on a handshake. That was my big mistake!

The store was up and running and profits were coming in every month. We were both able to put a fair amount of profit in our pockets and our inventory was growing. The business was a success. After about four months, that evil monster Greed came creeping in. Saul's wife wanted a salary drawing the amount from the profits generated by the business. "If your wife receives a salary for her efforts then I should also receive a salary for mine." I replied. "When I'm running around town buying for this store I'm neglecting my other businesses and incurring costs (gas and maintenance) which I have not passed on. We should stick with our original agreement or follow the adage that, what's good for the goose is good for the gander."

Saul said that they had learned enough about the business over the past few months to run it himself and he didn't need my help anymore.

The next time I went into the store, I discovered that the lock had been changed overnight and that I was now a persona non grata. When the store opened, I entered the building and confronted this ex-partner and his wife. If you ignore the fact that I overturned the desk they were sitting at and suggested that a female dog might have had some impact on their genetics, I would say I treated the situation with great diplomacy. The police were called in and I was regrettably informed that since I had no contract and the building belonged to Saul, I must depart and leave all my possessions behind.

Saul and his wife then tried to justify their actions by claiming that I was taking more money out of the business for purchases than I was actually spending. The claim had no foundation and the truth was the reverse scenario. Like the shoemaker who wears terrible shoes, I was the accountant that kept terrible records but I always erred in favor of the business. Everything I purchased was generating a good profit.

Having no written contract and relying on the handshake of a cheat, I was concerned there was no legal recourse. A lawyer assured me otherwise and took my case, took my money and finally informed me that after much study (surprise, surprise) that Saul was contesting my version of the events and with no written contract, we had no case. Screwed again.

After much argument, Marilyn convinced me that sending Saul to the intensive care unit of a local hospital was not an option.

"Go on with your life and learn from your mistake," she said. Saul will never know just how close he came to serious injury and that he was only spared because of a loving and forgiving wife. Mine!

An interesting array of customers

Over the years I have met people from every walk of life. Some had hard lives, some had privileged lives, some had confused and troubled lives and some had short lives. They came to my store to shop or just talk and they were never turned away.

My Urban African Safari

It was a cold, damp, blustery winter's day, the kind of a day that would freeze the balls off Margaret Thatcher when I received a call from a diplomat's wife. She told me that she and her husband were recent arrivals in Canada and that her husband's previous posting had been in Cameroon, West Central Africa. While living there, she said, they had acquired a number of African artifacts and souvenirs that they now wished to dispose of. She wanted to know if I would be interested in purchasing them and if so, when I could drop by their home.

After many years in the business I knew that that the early bird always catches the worm so I asked, "Would now be a good time?" "Come on over," she said, and I jumped up and rushed to my car moving faster than a diarrheic at a Mexican restaurant in Tijuana. They lived on an old tree- lined street in the heart of west end NDG in a majestic old Victorian home. I was met at the door by a striking six foot two raven-haired beautiful black woman dressed in a Ralph Lauren pants suit with matching designer jewelry and stiletto high heeled shoes that qualified as deadly weapons. Her distinguished six foot eight African American husband was standing by her side. The home was completed decorated in African motif which brought to mind the Rainforest Café my wife and I had visited at Downtown Disney. Standing there in my five foot six frame, I felt like a pale pygmy in a Zulu village. They immediately invited me to come in to have a seat at their kitchen table.

"Would you like a glass of pawpaw juice," they asked? Not wishing to offend or kill any chance I might have of making a purchase, I accepted their gracious offer not knowing what the hell pawpaw juice was and hoping it didn't taste like elephant piss. As I slowly drank what turned out to be a thoroughly delightful fruit drink, we started to talk business.

They told me that during their stay on the African continent they had visited many small villages and would often leave these villages with a gift or souvenir. Not knowing how to diplomatically refuse the generously offered gifts, they accepted them and over the years ended up with much more than they wanted or needed. Now, in a new country with a new life and new friends, they decided it was time to downsize. My name had been recommended to them by a mutual acquaintance.

They showed me a number of masks and bronze statuettes that were fascinating, disturbing and remarkably crafted. There was a three foot long bronze pipe with village scenes decorating every inch of surface area, a two foot high bronze statue of a chieftain sitting on a throne holding up the head of an enemy and a detailed bronze of a naked potbellied pregnant woman sitting spread eagled on the ground with her genitalia mesmerizing me like the open net in the last minute of a Stanley Cup hockey game. I was informed she was a fertility goddess. Most disturbing of all was an eighteen inch bronze penis with two native huts at its base and native village scenes decorating its shaft. It reminded me of that old proverb that it takes a village to raise a penis: I might be guilty of slightly misquoting that proverb.

After purchasing a small bow with poisoned arrows from them the man told me the story of how he and his wife had entered a pygmy village and after being greeted warmly by the villagers his wife made the mistake of entering one of the nearby native huts to get an impression of how they lived. After her intrusion into the home, the mood of the villagers immediately changed and a hasty retreat was decided on. They later discovered that because she had entered the hut the pygmies considered it defiled and after she left it was immediately burnt to the ground.

After a little haggling we decided on a price we both considered fair for my purchases and on my way out the door with my new found booty I noticed an interesting mask hanging on a small side wall. "Is that mask for sale," I asked. "Yes," the man said. "My wife hates it because it's covered by human skin."

"I'm afraid, in this case, I agree with your wife," I said. "I think I'll pass on your Silence of the Lambs mask. I love interesting items but even I have to draw the line somewhere."

After packing up all my new found treasures I headed back to the shop. My wife was less than impressed with my new purchases and after unpacking the eighteen inch bronze penis she made the uncalled for and rude comment that based on African standards I was coming up seriously short.

The rest of that day was devoted to pricing, displaying and selling some of my new found items.

Ironically, after returning from the pretty house with the death mask on the wall my first customer of the day was a young, athletic, good looking and slightly effeminate mortician and part time preacher that worked at the funeral home down the road from my store. After aggressively trying unsuccessfully to get me to reduce my reasonably priced African village penis he became agitated and told me to stick it up my ass. Watching my little fat face turn beet red as I struggled to swallow the comeback line I was choking on, he said, "You know, Frank, one day I'll be working on you."

Realizing that I was much older, overweight, and somewhat out of shape I believed he was probably right but I still considered the comment boorish and bad-mannered. He would have immediately been crossed off my Christmas card list if I had a Christmas card list. I'm a firm believer that we should never take anything in life for granted and that the fickle finger of fate can either kick or kiss you so I was not surprised when approximately five years later I had a good news/bad news sort of a day. The bad news was that the mortician had died suddenly due to a heart attack, the good news was that this old, overweigh and out of shape antique dealer got to handle his estate sale.

Approximately three months after my initial excursion into the magical and mystical world of African memorabilia, I received another call asking if I would be interested in adding to my existing inventory.

This time it was from the Pointe-Claire home of an elderly minister and his wife. Due to health considerations they had to leave their missionary work in the Congo to return to Canada. After our initial introduction we went into their so-called Jungle room. This room had a zebra skin table with six zebra skinned chairs. There were African bows, spears, knives, shields and blow guns with poison darts as well as ivory canes, tusks and figurines. In one corner of the room there were animal hides piled three feet deep. It was an animal rights activist's worst nightmare. One might wonder why this friendly, caring and loving couple, so concerned with saving the bodies and souls of men, women and children cared so little for the lives of all those trophy animals that were slaughtered to make up this huge offering. I wish I could say that I walked away leaving all the profit I would realize on the goods behind me but I'm afraid the good minister made me an offer I couldn't refuse and he led me sinfully into temptation. My rationalization was that the damage was already done and nothing I could do would give those beautiful animals their lives back so, what the hell, I still had to make a living. It's amazing how we can always justify the unjustifiable when personal gain is at stake. I probably lost a piece of my soul that day but business is business. Unfortunately my wife, the animal lover, didn't see it the same way and didn't speak to me for a week.

Somehow the word must have gotten out that I was interested in buying African art because the next thing I knew, this little five foot nothing, 350 pound African man comes into my store with two large garbage bags filled with tribal masks and fetish, fertility and ceremonial wooden statues. He told me he was the son of an African chieftain and that he travelled throughout Africa purchasing items to resell in Canada and the States. I acquired some of his wares and as he was leaving my store with slightly lighter bags than he came in with, I expressed my admiration of his royal status. He told me that it was no big deal because his father had about 50 wives and approximately 200 children and at the last family reunion everyone had to wear a name tags so that they could be identified in the sea of strange faces. I figured his dad must be a very athletic Mormon.

MAFIA BOY

One day as I was working in my original store a rather hyper young man walked in with a silver tea pot he had for sale. He told me that the pot was his grandmother's and that she had asked him to sell it because she was a little low on cash that month. After examining the pot I discovered something rather extraordinary about it. My price tag was still attached to the underside of the pot. It was a pot I had recently purchased and placed for sale in the new store. Excusing myself, for a moment, I went into my office, leaving my wife to stand watch. I called Mary at my second store to inquire if the young man I was looking at had recently been in and if he had purchased anything. The answer was yes and no.

Returning to the culprit, I asked him if he had any idea how my price sticker ended up on his grandmother's teapot. His reply was "Listen, man I don't know what the fuck you're talking about. It's my grandmother's, man, do you want to buy it or not?"

I told him that not only would I not buy it, he was lucky that I didn't call the police and have him arrested. He got lippy so I went around the counter and led him to the door without his grandmother's teapot. At the door, he took a swing at me and missed. I didn't.

Stumbling to the car that was parked in front of my store, he opened the front door and yelled, "I'm in the mafia and my family is all mafia. You're dead and your store is ash." My temper got the best of me, so I ran after him as my wife screamed: "*Stop, Frank, he could have a gun in the car.*"

Ignoring her, I reached the car just as he jumped in and peeled rubber. I had just enough time to take down the licence number and immediately called police to report a death threat.

Mafia boy, as I inaffectionately call him, ended up having a long criminal record and spent the next year in prison.

Years later, I read in the papers that he was arrested for a series of home invasions on elderly people and was heading off to prison once again. Only this time he was going away for a much longer term.

JIM AND EFFIE

Effie was a beautiful, but somewhat overweight, young Greek woman who somehow ended up married to Jim, a much older pudgy ex-con who had spent more time in jail than out of jail. Effie was the breadwinner of the family. She spent her days slaving away in a printing plant and her nights cooking and cleaning up after Jim.

Her family wanted nothing to do with her after her marriage to Jim and, by the process of elimination, he became her whole world.

Jim would come into my store and talk about the good old days when he spent money like it was going out of style because the next big score was just around the corner. You could tell by talking to him that he had no concept of the harm and pain he caused along the way. He saw himself as a Robin Hood that stole from the rich and gave to the poor. Anyone with more money than he had was rich and he was the poor.

Jim had nothing better to do than hang around my shop or the cockroach-infested restaurent next door, eating hot dogs and greasy fries and talking about how easy his life was with a wife taking care of his every need. He would buy the odd item in my store but, mostly, he just hung around waiting for his wife to finish work. Effie finally worked up the nerve to leave Jim and return to her family. The prodigal daughter had returned and the family was happy once again.

The greasy fries and hot dogs finally caught up with Jim, and he died of a heart attack.

The rich were a little more secure in their homes again.

THE HUNCHBACK OF NDG

She was a petite four feet tall lady with a pleasant smile, soft manner of speech and darting eyes which constantly roamed my shop looking out for any busybody who dared listen in on her conversation or pay too much attention to her transactions.

The hump on her back was quite prominent and her body emitted a pungent odor that had more to do with her medical condition or diet than her hygiene.

She was always neat, clean, lovable and annoying as hell. She scrutinized every piece she desired as thoroughly as a near-sighted proctologist performing a colonoscopy. While my wife or I stood and held our breath, she would ask a dozen questions about the origin of the piece, the materials used and the reason for every small flaw she discovered. Once she decided to make her purchase, a receipt had to be made out describing the item in detail. The final receipt agreed upon always had more information on it than most CSI reports on murder scenes.

One day I had to deliver a table to her small apartment in a Westmount senior facility. Once there, I noticed how suspicious she was of the other residents. They all seemed to ignore her presence. Without any urging on my part, she told me she had her deformity since birth but was fortunate enough to be born into a affluent family. Life was hard but not as hard as it could have been. She had a loving mother who took care of her every need and was always there to dry her eyes when she returned home from school after suffering the taunts and jeers of her insensitive schoolmates.

She still had a sister she kept in touch with. Although the family money was mostly gone, she lived in reasonable comfort and took great pleasure in every little treasure she found. At least they wouldn't hurt her.

RANDY ANDY AND JUICY LUCY

Andy was a British part time antique dealer living in Montreal whose only noticeable vice seemed to be his passion for 18th and 19th century Royal Worcester Porcelain and a turbulent and confusing relationship with his wife Lucy. Just about every antique dealer in Montreal coveted Andy's amazing Worcester collection and he loved to show it off. He was friendly, happy-go-lucky, fit and somewhat handsome with a one valium pill too many, laid-back outlook on life. His wife was ditzy and blond, with attitude and a high pitched voice that could be both amusing and excruciatingly painful at the same time. Andy was trusting—in my opinion, way too trusting.

One day he made the acquaintance of Tony, a British antique dealer, who was in Canada on holiday and they immediately hit it off so Andy opened his home and heart to him.

Andy and Lucy wined and dined Tony for three weeks and then arranged for him to liquidate Andy's mother's home back in England. Her recent death had left Andy with a large house fifty-two hundred kilometers away filled with antiques that had to be emptied quickly. Andy thanked the gods of the antique world for sending Tony as the solution to his problem. Tony said he would be glad to help out, so Andy accepted the generous offer and handed over the keys to his mother's home. Tony was also English, and everybody knows the sun shines out of every Englishman's arse so there was nothing to worry about.

After three weeks they said their sad farewells. Tony got on his plane and Andy never saw him, his mother's antiques, or the money generated by the sale of his mother's antiques again. So much for trusting your fellow countryman. On the plus side, however, the house did get emptied out.

Over the years Marilyn and I got to know Andy and Lucy pretty well, or so I thought. One day Marilyn decided to share with me some of the stories Lucy had been divulging to her about what she described as Andy's strange behavior.

My initial reaction to Marilyn's revelations was: "You've got to be kidding!" Unfortunately she wasn't, and it turned out that the stories were general knowledge among many in the antique trade and I was one of the last to know. It seems that my tough, hard ass, macho buddy Andy had a secret life. According to Lucy, Andy put on women's clothing, high heels and make-up and walked the streets of downtown's Boulevard St. Laurent at night looking for excitement.

I told Marilyn that I seriously doubted the story, and the fact that his wife was spreading it was both disturbing and baffling but then again everything's baffling in the crazy world of antiques and collectibles so I decided to turn the page. The page in this case was straight from a chapter of that sexual sadomasochistic book Fifty Shades of Grey and I doubt that even E. L. James, the author of that highly successful but questionable literary novel, could be as creative as Juicy Lucy was with some of her tales.

Among other things she told Marilyn was that instead of a birthday cake, Andy's recent birthday wish was for a threesome with a transvestite from an escort agency he knew and Juicy Lucy admitted to making the call. I asked Marilyn where they planned to light the birthday candles and how they intended to blow them out. Marilyn didn't appreciate the humor of my musings.

As the stories got wilder and wilder, they became more and more unbelievable. Next to Andy's colorful sex life I was living the life of a parish priest (sorry; bad analogy). To this day I don't know if any of the stories were true but what I do know is that the marriage eventually crumbled. Lucy ending up cleaning everything out of the house, including Andy's beloved Worcester collection while Andy was away so Andy got screwed once again and not in a way he would appreciate.

Andy eventually left the antique trade for a career as a construction worker. Hopefully one day he'll find a nice Indian chief, policeman, biker, cowboy and military man and start his own antique oldies-but-goodies band.

THE VIOLIN MASTER

Russian-born Canadian violinist Alexei has two major claims to fame

1- He played on stage with multiple award winner Itzhak Perlman

2- He played a second hand violin in my shop in NDG and the sound eminating from the instrument was so beautiful even the mice stopped to listen.

Alexei was married to a prominent lawyer from a well - established family and he had two teenage boys I refer to as Cain and Abel. Abel was a good kid. He gave his parents little trouble, did well academically and, for the most part, was a pleasure to be around. Cain, on the other hand, was a rebel without a cause. He would constantly get into trouble and create havoc at home. His philosophy was, "Let's eat, drink, and screw Mary, for some day, my parents will die, and I will be left with a shitload of money."

Alexei often dropped by the store to chat and check out any new art treasures or musical instruments that arrived. We would talk about life in general and Cain in particular. "I enjoy our little conversations," he would say, "They help redirect my mind from all that negative energy created by Cain's newest escapades. Whenever a trip to a Siberian Goulag is looking more attractive than the trip home, I drop by your store.".

One day, he came into the shop with a big smile on his face, so I naturally asked what the occasion was. "Cain's in a privately run, totally secure military college." he said, "he was dropped off over the weekend and there's peace in my home once again, Hallelujah."

"How the hell did you pull that off"? I asked. "Sound planning," he replied, "the KGB would have been proud."

Alexei told the story of how he enticed Cain out for a drive with a promise of generous gifts. When Cain went to get into the front seat of his father's car, he discovered it was already occupied by a rather large muscular man. Cain, a bright but troubled boy immediately suspected something was up. He had two options, walk away and miss out on a shopping spree or throw caution to the wind, climb in the back seat of the car and enjoy the ride. Having no experience resisting temptation, he naturally climbed into the back seat. Immediately, two robust gentlemen stepped out from behind a hedge, opened both back doors of the car and climbed in creating a neat little Cain sandwich. He started screaming blue murder, demanding to be let out but all to no avail. When he had finally settled down a bit Alexei informed him of his destination and the futility of resistance.

The location was a college on a desolate strip of land six hours away. Checking the rear view mirror, Alexei observed his son's face and knew he was planning his big escape at their first rest stop. Once free, the boy would then return home to his loving mother with pleas of, "Dad is being unreasonable. Please let me stay. I won't be any trouble."

As planned, after one hour on the road Cain complained he needed to go to the bathroom. Alexei pulled a tin can out from under his seat and said: "There you go, son. There are no stops on this run."

After dropping the boy off with his new commanding officer, Alexei returned home to a normal, quiet life. He went to visit his son often and, in time, the boy was allowed home on visits.

He loved his son dearly, he just didn't like him at that time of his life. Cain adapted to military school and turned his life around.

I don't see Alexei as often as I used to anymore. When he comes to my new store, we talk about old times and laugh about how difficult it must have been to piss in a tin can in a fast moving car.

BOB AND BETTY

They were two gentle giants who experienced more pain and heartbreak in their lives than I could possibly imagine and came through it with their dignity intact and loving hearts. Bob was a good looking, muscular man who worked long hard hours for a moving and storage warehouse. He would periodically receive gifts of unclaimed storage items from his boss as compensation for overtime hours worked. Betty, his wife, remained at home on a methadone treatment program for opiate addicts.

Many people place items in storage after a move and eventually forget about them or die leaving no record of the items. When payments aren't made, the moving and storage company eventually acquires the right to liquidate all stored items to help cover the warehouse cost. Some items prove to be junk and some prove to be treasures. A rather large police detective friend of mine I affectionately refer to as the Big Dick (a nickname not relating to any body part) purchased a container in a warehouse auction for $300 the contents of which he later sold for over $10,000. Big Dick made a big score. Bob was never that lucky.

He did, however, receive many interesting and attractive items which I would then purchase and re-sell. Over a period of time, we became friends and he told me the story of his troubled and abused childhood, running away from home at a very early age and being taken in by a merchant in Chinatown after he was found rummaging through a garbage container looking for food. Bob spoke perfect Mandarin, as a result of this episode in his life.

He told me he had served time in prison for killing one man and wounding two others in retaliation for the brutal rape of his first girlfriend.

After being released from prison, he met Betty at her work place. Betty was a prostitute and Bob was her number one customer. She was recruited into the business by her drug-dependant mother at a very early age and worked her way up to the position of madam. As a madam, she wasn't required to service any customers but she kept Bob on, so to speak, because she was falling in love with him. Bob worshiped Betty. He finally convinced her to give up her wild and dangerous life and marry him.

Betty, once a very beautiful, well-shaped woman, was now seriously overweight and walked around the house in a sedated state of mind. The years of abuse had taken their toll.

Bob never drank, smoked or did drugs, and was very health-conscious. He didn't need to work out to stay fit, his job was equal to ten workouts. He spoke softly, and even when angry, I never heard him raise his voice.

The lives of these two troubled souls consisted of renting movies to watch together at night after Bob finished work, ordering take-outs for supper, and just enjoying each other's company. It wasn't a great life but it was theirs. When Bob was lucky enough to score a half-way decent piece from the unclaimed storage, he would buy Betty a beautiful piece of jewelry. Over the many years that I have known Bob, I have never seen him buy anything for himself but he went through thousands of dollars on jewelry for Betty. She was still beautiful to him.

They were like two shipwrecked survivors desperately hanging on to a single piece of flotsam in the threatening waters that surrounded them. What kept them alive was their marriage, and the love they held for each other.

THE ANGEL ANGELINE

A middle- aged distinguished looking lady came into my shop carefully nurturing along her elderly French Canadian mother, and the overall demeanor of the two women immediately caught my attention. Little did I know that their beautiful faces and quiet distinguished airs camouflaged a sad secret. Still waters can have dangerous undercurrents.

After their initial introduction to my store, Angeline and her mother Elaine soon became regular customers. Their purchases were all minor but I was happy to accommodate them and always enjoyed their visits. They were friendly, helpful and polite. Their love for each other gave my store and my heart a magical warm glow. Angeline, I soon discovered, was married and holding down two part- time jobs. The mother told me that Angeline's husband was unemployed and relied totally on her income to keep the roof over their head, dinner on the table and liquor in the liquor cabinet. I asked if she needed extra work and her mother answered in the affirmative so I offered her a job. She accepted, started the next day and continued to work for me until the sad day she died.

Angeline was amazing with the customers. Her sense of style, her overall bearing and her smile were contagious and gave the store a badly needed degree of sophistication but unfortunately all was not what it seemed. I discovered her terrible secret one day when she came to work with a badly bruised face. When questioned she offered me a half-ass story about tripping and falling but her face and eyes told a different tale. I wasn't buying it but she stuck to her story and, not wanting too dig too deeply into her personal life, I accepted her explanation and to my everlasting shame let it be. Things went well for a while and although there was the occasional limp to her walk, pain in her arm and sensitivity around the rib area, there were no more facial bruises. Her mother continued to come to the store and one day I brought her aside her and confided in her my concern for her daughter. After some minor reluctance she opened up and confirmed my darkest fears.

Angeline's husband had a Dr. Jekyll and Mr. Hyde complex. To his friends and associates he was a good-humored, happy-go-lucky guy who wouldn't hurt a fly. His wife and mother-in-law however knew differently. In the Robert Louis Stevenson classic novel Dr. Jekyll and Mr. Hyde, Dr. Jekyll would go into his lab, mix up a deadly solution based on his secret formula and upon drinking it would become overcome with convulsive tortures and transform into the cruel, heartless monster. Angeline's husband could be a warm, affectionate, loving spouse but after drinking his Jack Daniels, Johnny Walker, Jim Beam or Captain Morgan concoction he would become overcome with convulsive jealousies, feelings of inadequacy, self-doubts and anger and transform into a hard hitting, soulless monster. He would abuse his wife physically, verbally and at times sexually and then pass out on the bed. On awakening he would cry out to his loving God and faithful wife for forgiveness with a promise never to drink the vile concoction again. Like Dr. Jekyll, his promise was always short lived. Angeline's mother had been trying for years to get her to leave him but Angeline was a forgiving angel and refused to leave. Like the little girl described in the Henry Wadsworth Longfellow poem, There Was A Little Girl, when her husband was good he was very, very good but when he was bad he was horrid. Economic uncertainty, fear, love or just blind acceptance kept her in her unfortunate marriage. I offered what support I could but unlike her husband I couldn't force it down her throat so I just made sure that her time in my store was peaceful and enjoyable.

I only spoke to her husband on one occasion and that was on the day after Angeline died. The phone rang in my store, I picked it up and was surprised when Angeline's husband identified himself and breaking down in tears said, "Angeline won't be in today, she dropped dead in the kitchen last night." I would have tried to console him but the fact was I really couldn't give a fuck about his feelings. Angeline's mother, now a shadow of her former self, came into my store approximately two weeks later to tell me her daughter had died suddenly and unexpectedly from a brain aneurysm. The funeral, she said, was a simple private affair. Angeline's husband was using her death as an excuse for a new drinking binge.

The monster now had no one to attack but his own reflection in the mirror.

TOM AND JESSIE

Tom

If there ever was a candidate for the AA program, it was Tom. In the more than twenty years I've known him, I can't remember a day that the smell of alcohol wasn't on his breath. I always believed that if he ever stopped drinking, the beer industry in this country could collapse.

With Tom you always knew that:

A) A cold beer was never far from reach.

B) He would never intentionally cheat or hurt anyone.

C) Drunk or sober, you could always count on him.

Tools were Tom's passion. Whenever a new power tool came into the store, he was there to buy it. He must have had nine circular saws, ten electric drills, eleven jig saws, twelve sanders and a partridge in a pair tree. What he was doing with all those tools was beyond me, but he was happy, and so was I. Tom was retired and bored at home so, eventually, he asked if I needed any work done around the store. After some hestation, I said yes. From that day on, we became close friends and continued to work together for almost twenty years. He was my cranky handyman and sidekick. We had many rip-roaring fights after which he would buy me a Coke or I would buy him a beer and all was right with the world again. Together we moved player pianos, couches, bedroom sets, dining room sets and every other piece of furniture imaginable. The general rule of thumb was, the heavier the piece, the more stairs we had to climb to deliver it. Tom could fix just about anything wooden but I had to keep him away from electricity.

One day, he offered to repair the light on my outdoor overhead sign. My mind must have been in la-la land that day because I said, "Yes, go ahead but make sure the power is off first."

After being assured that the power was definitely turned off, I watched as he climbed my aluminum ladder with a screwdriver in his hand. The next thing I see is Tom lit up like a Christmas tree falling onto the cement sidewalk below. The fall from the ladder broke the electrical contact that day and saved his life. As he sat on the sidewalk, with his back against the wall of my store, and that deer in the headlights look on his face, I called an ambulance. They kept him in the hospital overnight and wanted to keep him longer but he wouldn't hear of it. A cold beer was waiting for him at home. He signed himself out and came back to work.

Years of alcohol abuse finally caught up with him and he ended up in hospital undergoing surgery for a serious gastrointestinal tract disorder. I continued to pay him while he was off sick, so I was surprised when he turned up at the store one day looking like a death camp survivor asking if there was any work to do. I immediately sent him home.

Under doctor's instructions, he stopped drinking for a while, put on some weight and started to get his strength back. Soon, he was back at work and I was finding empty beer bottles hidden around the store. He ended up sick and in the hospital once again, underwent surgery and, this time, came out looking like a medical school skeleton. Somehow, he survived again, put on weight and insisted on coming back to work.

Cats may have nine lives but the cats surrounding my store all looked up at Tom in awe. I honestly believed that if there ever is a nuclear war the only survivers would be Keith Richards and Tom.

Jessie

In the Old Testiment's book of Job, the devil challenges God to test a righteous and holy man named Job. Job's possessions are destroyed, his family is killed, and he is struck down with a serious illness but his faith never wavered. Jessie reminds me very much of Job. She was a righteous and loving wife, a good mother, and a dear friend. The devil must have found her a real challenge because I've never seen a woman tested so cruelly.

Her husband Tom was an alcoholic and, although he never intentionally tried to hurt her, he did. The example he set for their children was not a totally positive one and all the money spent on booze could have been better directed at giving her the life she truly deserved. Her only daughter was sexually molested as a child by a visiting relative. The traumatic event left the child with low self-esteem which, later in life, led her into the heavenly disguised hell of drugs and alcohol. She contracted AIDS and died young. Her youngest son Darien suffered from Addison's disease. He was her golden boy and she loved him with all her heart. The family was having a little get together at a local restaurant and Darien was a no-show, so she became concerned. Jessie and the older son Tom junior, went to Darien's high rise apartment to see if he was alright. On entering his unlocked door on the 25th floor, they found Darien lying asleep in his bed with empty bottles of pills lying on the floor beside him and a suicide note asking forgiveness. Jessie, in a panic, shook him out of his sleep.

On awakening and discovering his plan was being disrupted, he jumped up, ran to the outdoor gallery and threw himself over. Tom reached out and caught him at the last minute but he didn't have the strength to hold on. Jessie was never the same after that. Young Tom eventually stopped blaming himself for not being strong enough to save his brother and got on with his life.

Jessie, somehow, survived the ordeal. I gave her a small job at my store to occupy her time and her mind. All my customers loved her. She was always helpful. If you needed advice on taking stains out of a tablecloth, fixing a doll, or making fudge, all you had to do was ask Jessie. In all the years I knew her, I never once heard her say a bad word about anyone, with one obvious exception (the man that hurt her precious daughter). Her only two vices were playing the poker machines at the local tavern (she drank Coke) and smoking.

At the poker machines, she would limit herself to once or twice a week, only play the nickle machines and stop when she lost ten dollars. She unfortunately didn't show the same self-restraint with her smoking habit and eventually died of emphysema. A precious angel was finally given her wings.

THE HOCKEY STAR'S SISTER

The call was to an apartment house in the west-end of town. When I arrived, I was greeted at the door by a sweet lady by the name of Mary Harvey. While checking out the items she had for sale, I noticed a picture of a famous Montreal Canadians hockey player on the mantel so I asked her about the picture. "Oh, that's my brother, Doug," she said, "That picture was taken when he played defence for the Montreal Canadiens."

Doug Harvey, considered by many as one of the greatest defencemen in hockey history won six Stanley Cups while playing with the Canadiens so I naturally asked if she had any hockey memorabilia for sale. "No," she said, "That's all gone, Doug was a bit of a drinker, you know." We completed our business, I thanked her and headed back to the shop to unload. She came to my store a few times after that with small items she had to sell. We always had a nice little chat before she headed out. It struck me how unfair it was that a hockey great should die in poverty when players of lesser degree were pulling in millions of dollars yearly. One day, she came in with a bag full of clothing and asked if I would be interested in purchasing them for $200 dollars. I told her that I wasn't interested. I could immediately see a sadness in her eyes that disturbed me. After talking with her for a while, I could tell that she was having money problems. I gave her the two hundred and told her to take the clothing back home. She gave me a gentle kiss on the cheek and promised to pay me back as soon as she could. She then exited the store, leaving the bag behind.

I only saw her once more after that. It was at an antique show where she was helping out a friend She smiled, told me how happy she was to see me and promised that she would return my money as soon as she got on her feet.

Approximately a year later, a lawyer came into my store and handed me a letter. "Jesus,"I said, "who's suing me now?" The lawyer said, "it's all in the document, sir,"and left. When I opened the letter I found a check for $200 and a note: FROM THE ESTATE OF THE LATE MARY HARVEY

THE FREELANCE JOURNALIST

Joe had been an on-again/of-again customer of mine for a number of years and, although he wasn't much of a talker, he struck me as a sensitive and intelligent kind of a guy. When he spoke, he spoke with a purpose and his knowledge of the mysterious and confusing world of antiques and collectibles was impressive. I asked him if he was a dealer and he told me that although he dabbled in antiques from time to time his main source of income was dealing in words. He was a freelance writer. He enjoyed my store because of his love of antiques and told me that as a writer he would often contemplate on the wonderful stories and secrets that were forever hidden within their structures. He said he wished he had the magical ability to make them talk.

Joe was an avid reader and appreciated the fact that I often had a brand new selection of hard cover books at enticing prices. One of our large daily newspapers would periodically call me into their downtown offices to make me an offer I couldn't refuse. Every publisher in Canada and the USA would send copies of their latest published books in the hope of a review. Some were selected for review and some weren't, but no books were ever returned to the publishers. Every six months the volume of these books would become overwhelming so as a bonus to their staff they would have a one-day four hour discount book sale. Any books that remained after the sale were offered to me at a greatly reduced price. I would drive to their office in my empty Ford F150 pickup truck and drive back to the store with my cab overflowing with new unopened books. Needless to say, nobody could compete with my prices and Joe looked forward to each sale.

Between 1934 and 1977 newspapers ran a comic strip called L'il Abner with characters named Mammy and Pappy Yokum and Daisy Mae Scragg. One of the characters of the strip was Joe Btfsplk, the world's worst jinx. He walked around with a rain cloud perpetually hovering over his head. Unfortunately on the last three occasions I met with my friend Joe he reminded me of cartoon Joe.

Our third-to-last meeting was at the store when he showed up on crutches with a badly damaged right leg. When I asked what happened he told me he was rummaging through a loft in an old barn looking for antiques when he went through the floorboards and ended up in the hospital with a concussion and a badly shattered right leg. Needless to say, he didn't find any antiques that day unless you count the old warhorse of a nurse that attended him at the hospital.

The second-to-last time I met him was at his home in the Cote St. Luc area. He was on his way as a war correspondent to

Afghanistan and had to sell some of his antiques in order to help finance his trip. He wasn't happy about the whole situation but he couldn't pass up the opportunity to make some real money and possibly get a book deal out of it.

The last time I met Joe was about a year and a half later when he came into my store seriously underweight, with a noticeable shake in his hands and his confident and optimistic attitude replaced with a look of desolation and despair.

I expressed concern over his appearance and asked him what had happened to him since our last meeting. He informed me that he had seen some very disturbing and horrific things while on duty in Afghanistan and couldn't get the images out of his mind so he was having trouble sleeping. Then he surprised me by saying: "Frank, I killed a man." He broke down in tears. I tried to console him while asking myself what the hell it was about me that made people think I could help them with all their problems. I seriously considered changing my sign to read: "Frank Hicks, antique dealer and part time psychotherapist."

When Joe got himself together I asked him exactly what happened. "It was probably the worst week of my life," he said, "and my nerves were frazzled. I came upon a hungry child on the street being propositioned by a Mullah who was offering him food for sexual favors. My mind snapped and I dragged the man around a corner, out of the child's field of vision and shot him in the head. It's that image that keeps me up at night." I told him what was done was done and there was no going back.

"The stress you were under caused you to react in a brutal way to a brutal situation," I said. "Although confession might be good for the soul, I wouldn't recommend it in this particular case. Instead of dreaming about the pedophile you shot, concentrate on the children you saved from this man's abuse. What you did was wrong, what he did was wrong and he would have continued to do it time after time after time. You destroyed one life, this monster damaged many. Turn the page and get on with your life. Self-recrimination at this stage will accomplish nothing."

I never saw him after that meeting, but I hope he's well, still writing and learning to accept the fact that sometimes life kisses you on the lips, sometimes it kicks you in the ass and sometimes it shoots you in the head.

DEAR JOHN

It was in a beautiful and grand ground floor apartment that I first met John.

The apartment was filled with wonderful antiques. John took great pride in showing them to me. There were old Victorian chairs, daybeds, and bookcases filled with rare and interesting books. "This was my great grandfather's" he said, as he showed me an old toboggan that would comfortably seat eight people, "and that was my grandfather's" he said as he handed me a gold-handled cane. When I admired a beautiful old wooden tall ship that was adorning the fireplace mantel, he told me how his father bought it from an old Quebec carver named Eugene Leclerc while on a trip to St. Jean and carried it safely all the way back home. On the wall of one room, I noticed a framed picture of an old printing factory. When I asked John about the factory, his smile faded and his eyes clouded over as he told me about the family's printing company. For generations, it had been in family hands. When John's father died suddenly, his untimely death left John at the helm of the company. Unprepared for such an important position, he watched as the company gradually failed under his leadership.

Remaining with his mother in their old family home, he nursed her as Alzheimers rapidly took over her life. John was now feeding and changing the woman who once fed and changed him. She eventually died leaving him in a big empty house he couldn't afford. The house was sold, the bills were paid, the taxman took his share, and what remained was split between John and his married sister.

When I met John, he was living off the money left to him and trying to write the great Canadian novel. Funds were running low so it was time to sell off some of his prized possessions. I purchased a few items that day. Every once in a while, he would call me back and each time I went back, I would see fewer and fewer items around his home.

He told me that a lot of his possessions went to auction and he was getting by on what I paid him and the auction proceeds. He was progressively going from riches to rags.

All good things must eventually come to an end and so it was with John's collectibles. His money ran out and he was put out on the street. With the help of some money I lent him, he found a very small garage-like apartment in NDG and started to work in a book store. He bought a bicycle and every Saturday and Sunday, he would bike around Montreal West looking for the small treasures that would make his life a little more comfortable and hoping for the big score that never came. He always had a beautiful smile on his face when he came to see me and usually a chocolate bar in one hand and a soft drink in the other. I would go outside, check out the latest purchase he had strapped to his bike, and tell him to go easy on the junk food.

One day, after a busy day running around to all the garage sales and estate sales in town, John went home and dropped dead of a massive heart attack.

I went to the service given for him at the local funeral parlor and I sat, watched and listened as his extremely wealthy sister stood up at the podium and told everyone what a wonderful, caring brother he was. I just shook my head and, sadly, went home.

BILLY THE BASTARD

It all started out one Friday morning with a house call to an apartment in Cote St. Luc. Most of my stories start out in this similar fashion because my life is a series of house calls, garage and moving sales, and the buying and selling of goods to everyday and some not so everyday people. To some that might seem a boring and mundane life because they've never lived it.

So I went to this house call in Cote St. Luc where I was shown a roomful of furniture, various decorative and household items and some paintings. Billy, the one in charge, told me he had to clear the house. "Everything goes to the man that quotes the highest price," he said. Normally, when I run into these situations I just excuse myself, turn around and walk out. I do this because I know whatever price I quote will be used as a barganing chip with the dealer that comes after me and I have no time to waste.

Among the junk, as I affectionately refer to it, there were three amazing antique items that didn't seem to belong with the rest, so I decided to take a wild chance. "Can I just buy one or two items?" I asked

"No," he said "It's all or nothing" That's when I decided to base my quote on the three items only. Their resale value,in my estimation, was at least six thousand dollars so I quoted three thousand, leaving myself a reasonable profit margin. The rest of the package could be sold off at bargin basement prices. He said he would think about my offer and get back to me with an answer.

The following Friday, a week later, I get a call from Billy informing me that my bid was the highest and to come pick up my purchases. When I arrived at the apartment, I looked everything over and noticed the three important pieces were missing.

"Is this everything?" I coyly ask.

"That's it," Billy replies.

"There seems to be something missing. I distinctively remember a large bowl and two figurines among the items you showed me last time."

"Oh, those," he said "I sold those to a dealer separately, I didn't think you would mind."

"You told me it was all or nothing when I last saw you, how much did this dealer pay for the three pieces?" I asked.

"He paid three hundred dollars, if you insist I will take it off the price you quoted me," he answered.

I then informed (Billy the bastard), as I now affectionatly call him, that the three thousand dollars quoted was for those three items alone and I had no interest in the remaining items in the room. When he heard this chilling news, Billy's face turned whiter than Casper the Friendly Ghost. I might have felt sorry for him if I wasn't so angry.

Wishing him a great weekend, I opened the door and returned to my store.

MARIETTE

Mariette was an ex-TV star who had worked on French children's programming. She eventually decided she had enough of the "little bastards" (her words not mine), and moved on into the antiques trade. Using the vernacular of the show business industry, I would describe her as a Mary Poppins/Wicked Witch of the West sort of personality. She was a voracious, vibrant, virile, vivacious lady who smoked like a chimney and swore like a marine. You had to love her.

The first time I met Mariette she was dealing with a customer at her little basement shop in the heart of Westmount, Quebec. The customer was offering her $100 on a $350 item and she was telling the customer to "Fuck off and don't come into my shop again." I was fascinated by her novel approach to customer relations so I quickly introduced myself as the antique dealer from down the street in NDG and she immediately offered me a glass of wine from the nearly depleted bottle under her counter. I told her I couldn't drink the last of her wine and she assured me that there was plenty more where that came from and not to worry.

I left the shop about two hours later with my head spinning and my stomach churning. The only smart decision I made that day was to leave my car behind and walk to Mariette's. I walked there but staggered back much to the consternation of my wife.

After our somewhat less than sobering introduction we would run into each other from time to time at garage sales, estate sales or at her shop or mine. She was an avid buyer and would often put together a package of items at my store, offer me a lower but reasonable price and then take them over to her store and mark them up at five to 10 times my price. I remember commenting on the price of a cedar chest she had for sale at $1200 dollars.

"Mariette," I said. "You'll never sell it at that price."

"I know," she said. "I don't want to sell it. I've rented it out at least eight times to movie and television production companies and they pay me a rental fee of 20 per cent of the selling price. Twenty per cent of $1200 dollars is a hell of a lot better than 20 per cent of $240 dollars and I'm careful I never cheat them more than their budget allows." How could I possibly argue with that questionable logic?

Over the years we did a few antique shows together and her antics during these shows were often both frightening and entertaining. She was, of course, always well supplied with wine and as the day got longer, she got tighter. When things went well she would break out in song, or play the circus pitchman using colorful and amusing dialogue to draw passers-by into her booth. But when things went bad they went very, very bad.

Comments she would usually take with a grain of salt would become fighting words. When a customer asked for a much better price she would snarl back: "Why don't you run down to that Salvation Army shop where I'm sure you'll find something in your price range." If a customer commented on what beautiful items she had while walking away without making a purchase, she would say: "If they're so beautiful, why aren't you buying? You must be looking for the ugly section of the show where I'm sure you'll feel much more at home." The familiar customer comment of: "There are a few things I find interesting, I might be back later," would be countered by: "I'll try not to hold my breath." But usually a simple "Fuck off" was sufficient. Needless to say, at the end of the show Mariette wasn't in the running for the Miss Congeniality title.

Mariette was crusty, capricious and captivating. Anyone who bothered to take the time to get to know her also discovered a loving and generous heart. She lived with her husband in the duplex they owned on West Hill Avenue in NDG. They lived downstairs surrounded by wall-to-wall dusty antiques while the upstairs was used for the storage of more antiques.

The first time I visited her home, I remember saying: "If you're not careful the combination of dust and your pack-a-day smoking habit is going to kill you, girl." Unfortunately, I was right and she was eventually diagnosed with chronic emphysema and tied down to an oxygen tank for the last few months of her life.

After her passing I became good friends with her husband who was also very ill. He was bedridden and not in the good way. This colorful and well-respected doctor who had instructed Canadian commandos on the technique of the quick and quiet kill during the Second World War was reduced to spending his days reading or watching television on a small 12-inch television that sat on a table at the end of his bed. I tried to convince him to sell some of his antiques at auction and use the money to buy himself a VCR, a big screen television, a top quality sound system and a comfortable bed, but he wouldn't listen.

Eventually I brought him my second- hand VCR to watch some of the old movies he so loved and a bottle of Irish whiskey that we could both enjoy. The whiskey unfortunately lasted longer than he did. I miss him, I miss Mariette and I also miss my old VCR and half-full bottle of whiskey which somehow vanished into thin air along with the house full of antiques.

THE BEAUTY QUEEN

As I stood behind the counter of my store, a beautiful young lady walked in looking for assistance. She had the figure of a goddess, baby butt skin, golden blond hair and eyes that could melt the heart of a process server. I damned near tripped over my feet as I rushed to be of help. She told me she was looking for a sideboard for her new apartment and I was luckly enough to have one. After purchasing the piece she made arrangements for delivery and left with the eyes of every male customer in my store following her.

The next day I delivered the sideboard at her modest but comfortable apartment and she was kind enough to offer my helper and me a cold beverage. We quickly finished our drinks, thanked her for her business and hospitality, and set out for the store.

A little over a year later, she returned to my shop and it was obvious that she had undergone a complete transformation. If she hadn't introduced herself, I would never have recognized her. The goddess figure had vanished with only the skeletal frame remaining, her hair had lost its lustre, her face was pock-marked and her eyes were hollow. She told me she was working in a Bonsai shop and had a beautiful Bonsai tree she wanted to sell. As I checked out the tree, I questioned her as to how her life had progressed since our last encounter. She told me she had a new boyfriend and everything was going well. I could tell by the sound of her voice and the sadness that was enshrouding her that she was lying. Lacking a green thumb and knowing as sure as death and taxation that the Bonsai would not survive my tender loving care I purchased it anyway and watched as she left my store. Only my eyes followed her out that day.

Approximately a month later, her boyfriend entered my store inquiring if I wanted to buy the sideboard back.

I could tell by his runny nose, dilated pupils and restless behavior that he was deep into the drug scene. There was little doubt in my mind as to what had became of the beautiful girl that once stepped into my store. I told him that the sideboard was his girlfriend's and that the only one I could buy it from was her.

"You can't do that, man," he said, "She blew her fucking brains out."

(What a difference a friend makes)

THE SABRINA SAGA

I was first introduced to Sabrina when she and Dick, her boyfriend, came into my store with a few items to sell. They were happy with the offer I made so after completing our transaction they suggested I visit them at their apartment on Queen Mary Road to make additional purchases. We made an appointment for 12 o'clock the following afternoon and I promptly showed up at 12:15 pm the next day, believing it fashionable to be reasonably late. After ringing the doorbell for approximately about five minutes I was finally rewarded by the sound of a female voice calling through the intercom. "Yes who is it?" she slurred out, sounding very much like Sleepy the Snow White Dwarf on drugs.

"It's Frank from the antique store," I replied. "We made an appointment yesterday,"

"O, good God," she said. "Just give me a minute."

Ten minutes later she buzzed me into the house and I was greeted at the door by the bride of Frankenstein. Sabrina was wearing an old rumpled-up and soiled dressing gown, her coiffure looked like Don King's electric hair on a power surge, her face was begging for makeup and she had purple Barney the Dinosaur slippers on her feet. I had obviously just gotten her out of bed. She asked me to be quiet because Prince Charming was still in bed sleeping. After showing me a number of items, we agreed on a price and just as we were settling up, Dick stuck his head out of the bedroom door. He must have been attracted by the smell of new Canadian 20 dollar bills. Much to my chagrin Dick and little Willy (Dick slept in the nude) walked up to me, took the money out of my hand, thanked me and said goodbye while Sabrina stood there and said nothing. As I headed to the door I asked Sabrina if all was right with her world, and she said everything was fine as she let me out the door.

Approximately a week later, coincidentally a day after welfare payment day, Sabrina came back to my store on a buying binge. The same woman who recently was ready to sell me anything in her home was now buying up everything in the shop. Noticing a bruising around her right eye I, once again, asked her if everything was alright. She told me that she had a fight with Dick and threw him out of the house. "Dick pulled out," she laughed.

Marilyn and Sabrina then got into a long male bashing dialogue while I quietly went on about other business.

Over the next three months Sabrina came a regular intervals into the store, buying and selling the odd thing and exhibiting a continuous spectrum of emotional highs and lows that confused, baffled and bewildered us.

Approximately two weeks before Christmas she came into our store with an invitation to dinner at her new apartment on Christmas Day. Using the excuse of my lifelong tradition of having Christmas dinner with family members, I thanked her for the invitation but regretfully declined her kind offer. Marilyn, on noticing her disappointment, jumped in with, "We can't do dinner but, if you like, we'll be stop by for a small lunch." Sabrina said that would be great and after she left I turned to Marilyn and asked, "What the hell did you say that for?"

"No one should have to spend Christmas alone," Marilyn said. "A couple of hours won't hurt us and might help her." Marilyn's words that day had the same haunting value as Mary Todd Lincoln's when she said, "Come on Abraham, a trip to the theatre won't kill you."

That Christmas we dined on reheated pizza and wine that was better suited for sprinkling on French fries than ingesting cold turkey from the glass. We ate the pizza with great trepidation and nursed our one glass of wine for the next two hours. Sabrina was animated, bubbly and chatty. She was obviously ecstatic to have guests on Christmas and happy for someone to share her life story with.

We discovered that she was an only child of a very wealthy father and highly sophisticated mother. Her father doted on her and gave her everything she wanted much to her mother's disapproval. She was her father's precious angel and her mother's spoiled brat. As she grew to adulthood she fell in love with a slightly older man that the mother disapproved of and the father suspected was a fortune hunter.

At this point of her story, she must have suspected my skepticism, so she produced her wedding album. The album showed pictures of, what looked like, a royal wedding and a reception in a hall fit for a Saudi oil sheikh. At the head table in the reception hall, with Sabrina and her father, was the then prime minister of Canada, Pierre Elliot Trudeau. This girl was for real!

After a year, Sabrina's new husband grew tired of her constant demands for attention, fancy gifts and expensive meals in high class eating establishments. After repeatedly hitting her, he hit the road, extorting money from her father on the way out.

Her father later retired and the stress of a demanding daughter and nagging wife, without the pressure release valve of an outside work environment, ultimately killed him.

Sabrina, much distressed over the death of her father whom she dearly loved, was further discombobulated by the discovery that his will left all his money and property to his wife, her estranged mother. She went from princess to pauper at the beat of a heart. The sudden transference from wealth to welfare left her physically, emotionally and mentally shattered.

Her irrational behavior polarized her from all her existing family members and she went from one failed relationship to another. No man would ever love her like her father did.

Marilyn and I got a taste of Sabrina's alter-ego when, after our short Christmas break, she called the store accusing Marilyn of stealing one of her rings at the Christmas luncheon. Knowing that Marilyn doesn't care for fancy jewelry and wouldn't steal a crust of bread if she was starving, I told Sabrina that her accusation was totally without foundation. "Take a good look around the house, I guarantee you'll find it" I told her.

Every day for the next two weeks, I would arrive at the store to discover anywhere from five to ten extensive phone messages from Sabrina rambling on and on about one complaint or another. Our compassion for Sabrina had opened a Pandora's Box and I was getting annoyed and concerned.

Three weeks later she showed up at the store in a happy buying mood and told me that she had found the missing ring. No apology was made, no explanation was given and no remorse was shown. I totaled up her purchases, made change, wished her a pleasant day and then turned my back on her. The next day I arrived at work to find eight new phone messages on my answering machine complaining about her mother, her life and whatever else was going wrong in Sabrina's bi-polar world.

Going home late that night after a particularly long and hard day, I sat back in my car seat, relaxed and turned on the car radio and Sabrina's voice came blaring out of my car speakers. It was a Freddy Krueger, Norman Bates moment. I discovered that my radio was tuned onto a talk radio station and that Sabrina loved hearing her voice transmitted over the radio informing the world of the celebrity status she once enjoyed.

Her calls continued and I continued to erase them without listening to them. They gradually became fewer and fewer and my life eventually went back to normal.

About six months later I got a call from Sabrina telling me that her mother died leaving her the house, its contents, her jewelry and all her money. She went from riches to rags to riches again. She told me she had sold the house quickly and rented another apartment in her present building to contain some of her mother's possessions.

Over the next two years she squandered her money away foolishly showering gifts on everyone she came into contact with. Everything from tickets for Canadian golf and tennis tournaments to music concerts. She ordered her food from the finest restaurants and hotels in town and had her meals delivered by taxi. The girl that once had everything but a normal life and a good head on her shoulders wanted to become the beloved princess once more.

The last I heard of Sabrina she was back to rags again, living on welfare and complaining of the bum deal life had dealt her.

DOUG & MARTHA

Everybody in the business of antiques and collectibles is aware of the various ways people go about making money in this trade. There are the:

1) Store owners (those owning a store of their own or sharing a store with other dealers)

2) Ebayers (buying and selling over the Internet and helping others buy and sell at a commission)

3) Pickers (buying by advertising in the classified section of newspapers, at estate sales, moving sales and garage sales and reselling to collecters, dealers and on the net)

4) Collectors (financing their collections by selling and trading)

5) Flea market traders

6) Auctioneers

7) Show people (dealers who supplement their income by trading their stock at the various antique and collectible shows in halls, shopping malls, fairs, church halls, and empty fields throughout Canada.

Doug and Martha fall into this last category. Martha has a full time job at a hospital with enough flexible hours to allow her the ability to travel around the country on weekends doing the various trade shows. Doug took an early retirement. He now spends his time searching for and selling memorabilia, consisting of everything from postcards to old magazines, lighters, advertising signs, toys, pocket knives, wine openers, catalogues, and calenders. Doug's taste in memorabilia sometimes borders on the bizarre. When you walk into their beautiful home and enter the living room, you are greeted by a large 18th century (1790) three by four foot mortuary sign hanging from the overhead beams on their ceiling. Anyone who doesn't know Doug might find this unique decorative item somewhat peculiar for a living room. When you get to know him and observe how he does everything in super slow motion, you'll understand his remarkable attraction to it. To Doug this sign is his equivalent of a Nascar banner hanging in a family room. Doug can best be described as a snail on prozac while his wife Martha does everything at warp speed and can be compared to the Energizer bunny on amphetamines. Talk about the odd couple. Doug is tall, slim, eats mostly healthy meals and just had a heart attack that I'm sure was caused by his heavy smoking because we can definitely rule out stress. He was lucky enough to survive and now he's back home sitting with that big mortuary sign hanging above his head. I told him once, "Doug, I got to tell you, that sign is a real downer at parties and after your heart attack you need positive influences around you and I'm afraid that mortuary sign over your head just doesn't cut it."

"It's a beautiful vintage sign," he said, "it's a reminder that we all must inevitably die." My response was that we all must inevitably have a bowel movement but I can't see a vintage sign proclaiming it in my living room of any positive value.

Doug's Party Sign

Over the past twenty years, Doug has purchased a lot of memorabilia from me and I have bought a few items from him as well. We have purchased estates together without ever arguing about who gets what and even moved to the same small town location. It's amazing what two people can accomplish together when greed doesn't enter the picture. There are a lot of good dealers in the market place and there are a few that I wouldn't piss on if they were on fire.

I consider Doug and his Energizer Bunny wife Martha among the good.

PETER THE PICKER

Peter would often come into my store, spot a piece he was interested in and start his usual whining routine attempting to get the piece at a better price. Sometimes, he was able to grind me down and sometimes he wasn't. If unsuccessful, he would leave my store pouting like a spoiled child. He was a likable enough guy and a hard worker who would often work on a small margin because his only overhead was his van and his gas. A driven man, he had a fixed amount he strove to acquire daily and would not give up the search until he had accomplished or beaten his target. At the end of each working day, Peter had a pocket full of money and no remnants of stock remaining in his van. That was his goal and nothing deterred him from it. Unfortunately, in his drive to reach his objective he didn't take the time to stop and reflect on the many lives he encountered along the way. He made the customary salutations when entering a home but they were shallow and devoid of any true feelings. His eye was always on the prize and complications brought on by human compassion only got in the way. I discovered this aspect of Peter's personality after I mistakenly recommended him to a middle-aged woman imprisoned in her home on a respirator. She had called hoping to sell me some of her household furnishings. After reviewing the pieces, I informed her that I was only purchasing antique furniture and bric-a brac at that time and her items, beautiful as they were, did not qualify. We spoke for a while and she told me about the health problems she was having and how she wasn't sure how much longer she had left. Dust was dangerous to her so she decided to clear her house of all excess furnishings and bric-a brac. She wasn't poor but she wasn't rich either, so she wanted to realize some money back on her purchases. She asked for my help. Wishing her success, I said I would see what I could do and returned to the store. I knew Peter's brother had opened a large second-hand store. Peter was helping him stock the store so I called him and set up a meeting with the woman.

The next call I received was from a very agitated woman stating that Peter showed up at her home, asked her the prices she wanted for the items in question, offered her a fraction of the asking price and then left the house in a huff because she refused his insulting offer and wasted his time. Her time, it seemed, didn't count. At no time during the exchange did he express the slightest concern for her health or her feelings aside from the cursory greeting when he entered her home.

I offered her my deepest apologies and made a vow never to recommend another dealer again as long as I lived.

THE LOVING MOTHER

Mrs. Gagnon was a very special lady with an amazing daughter. Once a week they came into my store looking for a magical antique to add to their already impressive collection and brighten up their day. The daughter loved costume jewelry and enjoyed painting so I would often trade a nice piece of my costume jewelry for one of her fine finger paintings..

Mother and daughter lived together in a modest apartment in a middle-class area, which was a far cry from the beautiful home they once occupied. Some people recognize quality and value when they see it, others need time to recognize its true value and others wouldn't recognize it if it sat on their face. Mrs. Gagnon's ex-husband, though not clinically blind, was selectively blind. When they married, they were madly in love and decided to share and seal that love with children. Their first child, a boy, was born strong and healthy but their second child, a girl, didn't work out as planned. The famous Scottish poet Robert Burn's in his poem "To a Mouse" said: "The best laid schemes o' mice and men gang aft agley." A simple but less eloquent translation of Burn's words is: "Sometimes shit happens."

Mrs. Gagnon's daughter was born with Downs Syndrome. The father, in his blindness, looked on his daughter and her deformed features as a monster; the mother looked upon her daughter as a precious gift of God. The father wanted to place the daughter in an institution, never to look upon her again, erase what he believed was a mistake and go on with his storybook life. The mother wanted to cherish their special gift, accept their new challenging life with optimism and unconditional love and keep the family unit together. The mother's selfless devotion to her daughter was considered a betrayal by her husband and his inability to love the child and face the many challenges of bringing up a child with Downs Syndrome eventually lead to divorce. Mrs. Gagnon lost her home, her husband and her privileged life.

Yes; sometimes shit happens.

When I first met Mrs. Gagnon, her daughter was a fully-grown woman working at a provincially subsidized company that specialized in the employment of handicapped Canadians. She was a very happy lady with a contagious smile. She adored her mother and her mother adored her. Mrs. Gagnon's son drew strength from his sister and went on to become a very successful businessman.

One day, Marilyn and I were invited to dinner at their home and we happily accepted. The dinner was exceptional, cooked by both mother and daughter, the company was delightful and the ambience magical, with precious antiques surrounding us. We offered to clean up after the meal but Mrs. Gagnon wouldn't hear of it. Her daughter, she said, loved being helpful and would be offended if we took her job away from her. She might have a mind of a child but she had the heart and the soul of a saint.

In all my years in business I have never seen two people closer or happier together. Yes, Mrs. Gagnon lost her home, her comfortable income and her privileged lifestyle but what she gained she considered of much more value. Mrs. Gagnon eventually died a happy woman but unfortunately her happily married successful son felt ill-equipped to provide a home to his sister and she ended up in an institution. Somehow he and his wife were able to provide room in his happy home for the mother's antique collection.

Unfortunately, as Robert Burns said, "Sometimes shit happens."

MILLIONAIRE MIKE AND MELBA

Mike and Melba were good customers, good friends and good people. Melba, a cancer survivor, spent her time working with Hope and Cope, a volunteer non-profit organization dedicated to helping cancer patients and their loved ones through the physical and mental healing process. She also spent time looking for vintage jewelry to sell at the various antique shows around town. When not working for Hope and Cope, or working trade and antique shows, she ran a small store from the basement of her home where selected customers were invited to check out her display cases filled with her beautiful costume jewelry.

Mike was a regular guy, an ex-chef who now dabbled in organizing estate sales. He always had a smile on his face that reflected his happy-go-lucky sense of humor and joie de vivre. I was always glad to see him with his latest joke or crazy story about what was happening in his life. He was a good buyer and always negotiated in a reasonable manner, bearing no ill-will, no matter what the final outcome was. Mike and Melba made a modest living and were cherished by all.

One day, Mike came in informing me that his basement had just flooded destroying a number of his and Melba's possessions and highlighting a major foundation problem that existed in their home. He had no idea where he would get the money to make the necessary repairs. I sympathized with his plight and offered up the hope that his next estate sale would generate enough money to pay for the work that had to be done.

"From your lips to God's ears." he said as he left my shop.

A week later, as I sat on my comfortable reclining chair enjoying a late night hot cup of tea with Marilyn and watching the late news on TV, I see Mike at a press conference answering questions about his plans for the ten million dollars he just won in the provincial lottery. After tearing off my sweatshirt now soaked in steaming hot tea and applying cold water and burn ointment to my chest and stomach, I attempted to call Mike and Melba to offer my congratulations. The line was impossible to get so I gave up and put my now bruised and battered body to bed.

The next day I tried calling again and gave up in frustration after hearing one busy signal too many. A number of days later I decided to make one more attempt and dialed the number a last time. "Hallelujah" I yelled," as the phone rang, "success at last". After two short rings, an unrecognizable voice comes on the line proclaiming, "This is Mike and Melba's personal assistant, what can I do for you?"

"Personal fucking assistant, you got to be kidding," I said in frustration as I hung up the phone.

I saw Mike approximately two months later as he pulled up to my store in a brand new BMW convertible, wearing designer cloths, Ray-Ban sunglasses, a new Patek Philippe watch, Italian loafers and a scarf tied around his head.

"Mike," I said, "what happened to your head?"

"Do you have any idea how much this designer scarf cost me?" he said.

"Not really but I'm guessing a lot more than a bandage," I replied. His reaction to my comment told me that he had obviously lost his sense of humor so I changed the subject.

"Where have you been?" I asked.

"It was getting too crazy at home so Melba and I went to stay at the Ritz for a couple of months," he said.

He went on to tell me that he was having his old home fixed up for his son to live in and was moving to a much larger home in an affluent section of town. He looked around my shop, found something he liked and to my amazement asked what my best price was. Knocking a few dollars off, what I knew to be a reasonable price, I realized that those few dollars meant more to my financial well-being than his yet he was the one asking for the cash discount. I knocked the price down to show him that I didn't give a damn about his new financial status and would continue to treat him as I always treated him.

Now numbered among the affluent in society, I regretfully concluded, he developed the mindset that the poor and middle class should be kept in their place. We said our goodbyes and off he went to greener pastures.

I bumped into him a few more times over the following years and discovered that his new net worth had resulted in some family squabbles, marital problems, an inflated sense of self-importance and rejection by his new wealthy neighbors. It seems they had a low opinion of the nouveau riche. Eventually, he moved into a slightly more modest home with neighbors that judged you more by the size of your heart than the size of your bank account and lost that insolent attitude he had acquired along with the new-found wealth.One day he came into my store laughing. He came in to show me the new remote control fart machine he had recently purchased, featuring a repertoire of 15 disgusting fart sounds. Unimpressed as I was with the fart machine, I was glad to see the old Mike I knew and loved was back. Melba must have taken her attitude shot along with her flu shot the year they won the ten million because the money virus, somehow, never affected her.

THE WHITE WITCH OF THE WEST

Sarah didn't have a black dress, peaked hat, long crooked nose or bright green eyes but she was a witch all right. She told me so.

"Don't be so hard on yourself," I said, "You're a wonderful person and one of my favourite customers."

"I'm not being hard on myself," she stated, "I'm proud to be a witch."

"Sorry, I thought you said bitch," I answered.

She laughed and went on to explain that she was a white witch who believed in the power of positive thinking and good works. She and other members of her cult would get together

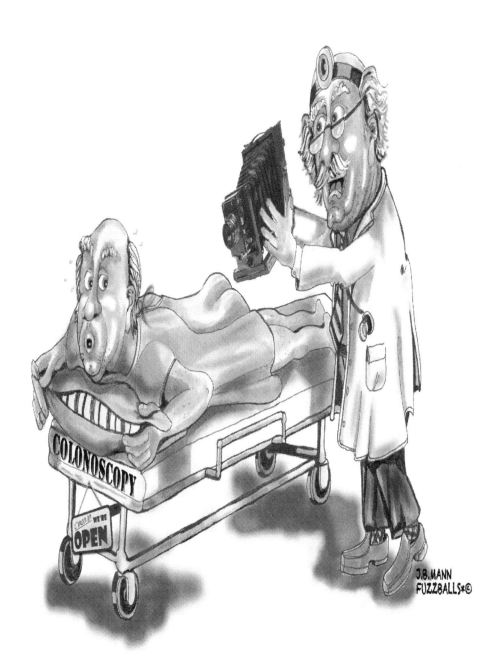

..."THIS IS GOING TO HURT"...

periodically during a full moon to give thanks to the planet earth and all its wonders. She did mention that some of their meetings were conducted out in open fields and backyards where members would strip off their worldly belongings and dance naked in a circle celebrating life. "I'm not into frolicking naked outdoors," I said, "Canadian winters in Quebec are much too cold, and in the summertime the mosquitoes would eat the ass off me."

Sarah didn't care for new things. She loved antiques but only antiques that gave off good vibes and had a long happy history associated with them. I told her that I also loved antiques but enjoyed some of our modern-day conveniences.

"Having a colonoscopy with a new fibreoptic camera is much more comfortable then those old Kodak box cameras," I jested.

She told me she could tell if a piece had a positive or negative aura just by touching it. "That ability must come with being a witch," I replied, "The only way I can determine the positive or negative aura of a piece is through observation. If it sells and puts money in my pocket, it's positive, if it sits in my store forever, its negative."

Sarah was a loving, kind and generous person so I didn't much care what she called herself as long as she never changed.

Over time, Marilyn and I became good friends with Sarah and her family. Her husband, we found out, was in the jewelry business and her brother was a well-known television personality. She had three young children.

Unfortunately, Sarah's ability to detect negative and positive auras didn't work too well at home. One morning Marilyn and I were having an early morning tea and blueberry muffin at our favourite Tim Horton's coffee shop when we noticed Sarah's husband Steve leaving the motel office next door with his arm around a beautiful young girl. They walked into the coffee shop smiling, laughing and kissing. Upon entering, Steve noticed Marilyn and me sitting at our table. The beautiful after glow on Steve's face suddenly turned deathly white.

He quickly turned around and flew out the door with his young friend protesting, "but Stevey baby, I thought we were going to have a coffee."

Marilyn was upset and wanted me to call Sarah and tell her about Steve's philandering. We talked about this for a while and I said.

"Let's keep this information to ourselves. We don't want to cause a marriage break-up, especially one with children involved."

Sarah's powers of perception eventually kicked in a few years later when she kicked Steve out on his ass.

She went on with her life bringing up her children and eventually meeting a handsome and charming Frenchman who she later married.

My white witch got her magic back.

ALBERTO AND AMBER

Amber first came into my store and my life approximately 25 years ago accompanied by her good friend Lolita. It was one of those days were everything was going wrong and paranoia was the mindset of my day. The fickle finger of fate can either fuck you or French kiss you and I wasn't being kissed that day. I was beginning to feel that life was, as my good friend Will Shakespeare once said, "A tale told by an idiot full of sound and fury signifying nothing." The sound and fury part of my life was just about to go into overdrive.

Amber was from Venezuela and there was no denying the hot Latin blood that flowed through her five feet nothing, 100 pound well-developed little frame. She hit my store like a Texas tornado with her tongue rattling off like a Thompson sub-machine gun in a 1920's gangster movie. Her exhilarating zest for life, I soon discovered, was contagious.

She ran all over my store acting like a kid in a candy shop and commenting on everything she discovered while her quiet, subdued friend Lolita followed saying, "Yes Amber, No Amber, and Ok Amber."

"Jew have such a wonderful store," Amber said to me in her unique effervescent Latin sort of way. The first thought that went through my mind was what makes her think I'm Jewish and why is this cute little imp suddenly turning all racist on me. She followed up with," Have jew been here long," and I suddenly realized her Venezuelan English accent was converting all you's to Jews so from then on I just ignored the slight speech impediment. Amber and Lolita were good customers that day and continued to be good customers and good friends ever since.

Amber's husband Alberto, I discovered, owned an auto repair shop and a number of properties around the NDG region. Pasqual, Lolita's husband, owned one of the most popular NDG restaurants and was an ex-professional hockey player. Alberto and Pasqual had many things in common, they were both Italian, they were strong family men with loving wives and two beautiful daughters, they both enjoyed cycling and they both came into my shop pissed off at the amount of money their wives were spending. I told them, "Sorry boys, your wives, your problem; I have a hard enough time trying to control my own. You're not the first husbands to be angry with me and you won't be the last. When I was younger a couple of husbands even threatened to shoot me and I didn't even own a store then." Alberto and Pasqual both laughed and we soon became close friends.

My wife and I became particularly attached to Alberto and Amber as well as their children sharing many meals together both at their home and at ours. Amber kept buying up my store only now it was to the chorus of Alberto's voice singing out, "Ah Amber, what do you need all this for, you're breaking me. Come on Amber, we already got enough Christmas ornaments, our place looks like an explosion at Santa's workshop. Amber, I'm telling you one last time, Amber we don't need it." Amber ignored his pleas for sanity and I would just smile and count out Alberto's money.

Marilyn and I helped get Amber her first shelter dog, a tiny little Shih Tzu named Chip. This cute little Shit, as I would later name him, ended up biting Amber's daughter in the face causing an injury that required six stitches and then he damn near took my hand off. Our friendship survived this minor mishap and surprisingly so did Chip. Alberto decided, after some contemplation, to "leave the gun and have a cannoli" (misquote from the movie The Godfather).

With a little training, Chip ended up living a happy, loving and well-behaved life with the family. More tears flowed when Chip died of old age than flowed on, what I always referred to as "the day of the six stitches."

I held a high level of respect for both Alberto and Pasqual, they were young men who started with little' but through hard work, personal risk, perseverance and dedication built up businesses that not only supported them and their families but families of those employed by them. They did this without any government help or handouts.

Amber and Lolita, despite both having jobs, Amber as a school yard monitor and Lolita working in the family restaurant business, were both instrumental in creating a happy family life with a deep-set system of values. Some of their children are now on their way to having children of their own.

Hopefully they will all continue to shop at my store and I will have the opportunity to piss off another new generation of husbands.

PECULIAR PERCY, THE PATRICIAN

Peculiar Percy, the Patrician, is a classy eccentric hoarder. Although Percy couldn't fight his way out of a wet paper bag, he holds a 10th degree black belt in hoarding. His third floor two-bedroom walkup apartment in downtown Montréal is piled ceiling high with cardboard boxes. The boxes are all filled with quality antiques that have been lovingly wrapped with the greatest care. A tubby guy like me would have a difficult time getting around his apartment but if you weigh 110 pounds soaking wet and cover your body with KY gel you might just be able to work your way around the rooms by sliding sideways.

When not buying new antiques on Kijiji, Craig's list, eBay or some other internet site, Percy can be found shopping in my store or one of the many other antique stores in and around Montreal. According to Percy everything he buys is junk and then it magically transforms into a quality item once in his possession. Percy has been a customer of mine for over 20 years and throughout the 20 years, we've had a great time playfully playing tricks and trading insults with each other.

We both have broad shoulders and thick skins so feelings are seldom hurt and one never steps over the line. We came damn close to the line on many occasions but never stepped over it.

Unfortunately Percy's childhood was not an easy one. After being given up by his mother he was bounced from foster home to foster home until he finally settled into a reasonably happy home where he felt slightly less than an outsider. Despite his troubled childhood he grew into a well-adjusted, well-educated professional holding down a responsible job and living with a guy so effeminate he made Truman Capote look butch. Percy's job as manager of a multi- millions dollar pension fund comes with a stress factor equal to that of resort manager at an asshole convention.

Percy has impeccable taste. Every time he walks into my store he has the amazing ability to dowse right up to my latest purchases and select a number of my finest items. He then spends 10 minutes belittling them in a feeble attempt to negotiate a lower price. Once his denigration process is over, he starts his negotiations on a bulk-buying basis for the so-called derelict items. After he left my store my ass would always hurt and that's peculiar because I'm reasonably sure he never came close to it. Being a slightly vindictive man I would always find a way of getting even. Once when my store was filled with people and Percy was fiddling away somewhere in the back of my shop I yelled out to him," Percy, your book dealing with erectile dysfunction just came in." My wife almost choked and he immediately tried to become inconspicuous, which was a little difficult with a store full of people staring at you.

Over the years my wife and I became great friends with Percy but we never quite warmed up to his houseguest. Marilyn was a tomboy as a child and never grew out of it and I'm a typical male with interests in martial arts, wartime memorabilia, hard-hitting sports and action movies. Percy's house guest loved dolls, pretty fabrics, and interior design and Broadway musicals. Needless to say we had little in common. Percy, on the other hand, had a quick wit, a love of antiques, a sharp analytical mind and a great sense of humor. Marilyn and I both loved him. He would often come to dinner at our home and when he did, it was always fun.

I remember one evening when our guests were Percy, Mike (a trader in military collectables), his wife Judy (a stock trader), Gerdy of Gerdy's Rescue (a dog and cat rescue) and her retired friends Judy and Roger. We had all just finished a great meal and just before dessert Percy excused himself, left the table and returned minutes later with an extra-large box of gourmet candies, which he immediately opened and placed on the table. Percy knew I had a serious sweet tooth and when buying antiques would often bribe me with candies to help sweeten up the deal.

When he sat down I thanked him for his generous gift and mentioned that I had unfortunately forgotten to put cream out for the coffee. Acting the gentleman as I knew he would, he graciously offered to fetch it from the fridge. As he left the dining room I immediately emptied all but one of the candies onto a clean plate, hid the plate and then awaited his return. He was out of the room but a minute and upon returning sat down, made a few polite remarks about the meal and quietly glanced over at the nearly empty box of candies. Noticing his look of consternation I immediately cried out joyfully, "Look there's one candy left," and quickly picked it up and ate it. The look on Percy's face was priceless. It was a Kodak moment and I didn't have my damn camera at the table. The other guests almost pissed themselves trying to keep a straight face while I acted as if nothing unusual had happened. Revenge is sometimes sweet. After a proper interval I took out the hidden candies, everyone erupted with laughter and Percy, smiling, shook his head and quietly started planning his payback. The next time he came to our home he brought chocolate squares and I spent the night in the bathroom. Revenge sometimes comes in sweets.

Percy is retired now. He spends most of his days enjoying downtown Montreal, admiring the beauty that surrounds him and wondering what the hell the younger generation sees in disposable sawdust and glue furniture, ugly yet practical dishes and assembly line collectibles.

After more than 20 years we're still good friends (at least I hope so after he reads this piece), but with the march of time we're both getting older so it's anyone's guess as to which one of us will have the first opportunity to put the whoopee cushion in the other one's coffin.

THE SURVIVORS

One of the greatest examples of man's inhumanity to man was the holocaust, and my many years in the antique business have brought me in contact with some of the amazing men and women who survived that horrific and brutal period of world history. What surprised me was their ability to laugh and love after the horror they endured. Some have proudly shown me their concentration camp tattoos as proof of their ability to survive whatever obstacles life threw in their path. I'll always remember the unique sense of humor of one enchanting holocaust survivor. On entering her apartment I immediately noticed that it was filled with Jewish documents, photos, memorabilia and souvenirs from Israel. Over tea she told me the story of how she and her husband survived the German concentration camps and came to Canada to build a new and happy life. After tea she proceeded to show me the items she had for sale and we went into a rather lengthy negotiation process. A mutually agreeable price was finally agreed upon and as I started to pack up she turned to me and said, "You're a real Jew you know." I did a double take! My first thought was, "Am I hearing right? Did this wonderful old Jewish woman just make an anti-Semitic remark? ". "No" I replied, "I'm a Roman Catholic. What makes you think I'm Jewish?". "You're obviously a good business man and know how to strike a fair deal so naturally I assumed you were Jewish." she said with a smile. I smiled in return, thanked her for her kindness and walked away realizing that it's not necessarily the words that cause the offense but the intention behind those words. Some compliments are disguised insults and some perceived insults are, in fact, wonderful compliments.

I remember another time when I was called to the home of a retired Doctor and his aging wife. They were both childless, in poor health, and desperately needed to downsize. After going through their home and making offers on a number of items I eventually noticed a beautiful Nymphenburg figurine locked safely away in a china cabinet. I asked if the figurine was for sale and after some hesitation they said yes but only if I would guarantee that it would end up in a good home. I promised that I would and once a price was agreed upon they proceeded to tell me the history of that wonderful piece. The figurine, they said, once belonged to a young Jewish girl fleeing Nazi persecution. She held this beloved family heirloom firmly against her chest as she ran across a desolate snow-covered border crossing knowing she could be shot at any time. Fortunately she escaped and eventually ended up in Montreal, Canada. While in Montreal she became very ill. This doctor and his wife treated her and helped bring her back to good health. As payment she offered them the only thing she had of any value, her precious figurine. They refused but she wouldn't take no for an answer. Her pride wouldn't allow her to accept charity so this courageous, loving and noble girl paid them with the item she held most dear.

The figurine has been lovingly kept in my home for close to 25 years now. I hope the doctor and his wife would approve.

On the other end of the spectrum, a contact of mine arrived at my store with a beautiful bronze Art Deco lamp and a German ceremonial WWII dress sword that he wanted to sell. He found the items in a small home in Verdun, Quebec. The home, he said, was filled with beautiful European furnishings, decorative pieces and paintings shipped over from France at war's end. The inhabitants of the home, a man and his wife, reminisced with him over drinks about their old life in a beautiful French castle. That life, unfortunately for them, ended when the war ended and they were forced to leave France. The Nazi sword he purchased was hanging on the wall of their living room. It didn't take great powers of observation to arrive at the conclusion that they were, most likely, Nazi collaborators that had to flee France along with the Germans

You meet all kinds in this business, the good, the bad and the ugly.

THE RACISTS

It was a dark, damp, dismal and disappointing day when this rather good looking young man and his rather pleasantly portly wife entered my store looking for Paragon china. One glance at them and their butter-wouldn't-melt-in-their-mouth attitude and I quickly came to the mistaken conclusion that they had a degree of sophistication. This impression was reinforced when she mentioned that she had, until recently, worked for a world renowned Canadian chanteuse and philanthropist.

Naturally I wondered why she left her job and the possible reason soon showed its ugly head. I discovered that first impressions are not necessarily the right impressions and in the case of these two seedy characters, my first impressions were way off base. When I questioned her as to why she collected Paragon china she said, "I love it because my mother loved it. Like most children I followed in my mother's footsteps." I found this to be a fairly honest and sincere answer and then made the mistake of following up by asking what her husband collects.

"I collect Nazi memorabilia," he said proudly. This statement alone didn't shock me. Over the years, I've met many collectors of military memorabilia, which also includes Nazi items, and most of them were respectable and caring people with a passion for historic preservation. It might be an ugly part of world history but there is no denying that the Second World War was a major part of world history. I informed him that I didn't have any military items on hand at the time but it wasn't inconceivable that I might have some in the near future. I told him about an Argentine couple that once came into my store with a box full of German military items for sale.

"There was a flag, an armband, a Nazi membership pin, medals, a short whip and a SS pass book signed by Heinrich Himmler," I said. "I took them home with me but didn't like the energy they generated in my house so I brought them back to the store and sold them to a collector I knew." What they said next shocked, disappointed and disturbed me and I witnessed the metamorphosis of a seemingly harmless couple into vicious cold-hearted racists. Not all monsters wear masks and carry axes, after all.

"Bad energy? That's just silly," his wife said. "Nazis aren't the hooligans they are portrayed to be." The husband then joined in.

"My wife's right. Hitler and the Nazi party helped turn Germany around. They pulled Germany out of a depression, restored German pride and created jobs. They took money from the rich to give to the poor."

With my usual diplomatic tact, I replied: "Of course, you're right, now that I think of it, Hitler does look a little like Robin Hood only with a silly mustache .Why don't you stick your head up your ass and take a nice big sniff, because that shit your spreading really stinks. You obviously can't smell it because you're too close to its source. I'll bet you also believe the Holocaust never happened."

"You don't believe all that crap in the Jewish media about six million Jews killed do you?" he challenged me.

I replied: "One was too many; six million men, women and children was an atrocity. Why am I even talking to you about this? I bet you still believe that the world is flat, Bernie Madoff was innocent and the Apollo moon mission was a hoax. That shit-for-brains attitude of yours will get you nowhere. Before I moved to Hudson, my store was in the NDG area and most of my customers were from Cote St Luc and Hampstead, two nearby predominately Jewish areas. I have met Holocaust survivors and spent a good deal of my life interacting with Jewish people. Many of my old customers are now old friends. Perhaps you would rather believe lies than believe in the truth because the truth is disturbing and ugly. Germany was an educated society prior to the Second World War and yet it was enticed into accepting the Nazi party, their propaganda and their barbaric behavior. This truth shows what mankind is a capable of under the right or wrong conditions and that profoundly scares me," I confessed.

"You're a weak man," he said, "and because you are weak, you scare easily. Be afraid of the Jewish Defense Organization and the Zionists if you are going to be afraid. Strong, well-educated, pureblooded people like me should be welcomed not ridiculed," he argued.

"You're making the common mistake of confusing education with intelligence. I've known many educated people in my life but few truly intelligent people," I stated.

"I believe that the scale of racism has stupidity on one side and racism on the other, the greater the weight of stupidity, the greater the height of racism," I continued. "Please be careful because you and your wife are on the scale on the side of racism and when you step off you have a long way to fall."

They both left my store and strangely enough, I never saw them again. I figured it must be my deodorant.

THE OPERA SINGER AND THE PLAYER PIANO

My upright player piano fiasco started when I purchased an 850 pound beauty from an elderly woman living on the second floor of a Lachine, Quebec duplex. The events of that day are forever chiseled into my mind and body. Some people tie a string around their finger as a memory aid and then quickly forget what it was they were supposed to remember. The scars on my left arm are my constant reminder of that day.

What sold me on the piano was the beautiful sound that emanated from it during its test run. For that first test I chose a piano roll titled "Born To Lose." As I sat on the piano bench, pumping the foot pedals and running my fingers over the ivory keys I felt like a white Ray Charles. My wife, always ready to shatter my illusions, told me I looked more like a fat Elton John. She also stated that at my current weight I was definitely born to lose and that the job of moving the piano would most likely kill me. I ignored her petty comments and decided to go full speed ahead with the purchase. To help with the momentous moving task I hired two guys that I shall henceforth refer to as Grumpy and Dopey, Grumpy had a mouth like a Calcutta sewer and his strange sidekick Dopey, when not doing small side jobs, spent his time booby-trapping his house for protection against thieves. The fact that there was nothing worth stealing in his home did not dissuade him. Any self-respecting thief would probably leave money in his home after breaking in. That is, of course, if he didn't end up with a hand full of shattered glass, a nail driven through his forehead or badly mangled testicles resulting from a shotgun blast.

So these were my helpers as I tried getting the piano out of the house and into my truck. The tricky part of the move was the ninety degree turn you encountered after descending the top four stairs. After that it was smooth sailing, if you didn't kill yourself trying to get down a steep flight of stairs and out the door. To get the piano past the first hurtle, the person or persons at the top would have to lift their end until the piano was at a sixty degree angle. Grumpy took one look at the task ahead and said, "You'll never get that mother-fucker out of this place."

"It came into the house by this stairway so it should leave by this stairway and please watch your language." I said as I glanced over at the beet red face of the old woman. "OK, but this cock-sucker is going to be a killer," Grumpy replied. At that point the woman left the room.

I told Grumpy once again to watch his language and of course his response was, "What's wrong with my fuckin' language."

Dopey, finally waking up from the stupor he was in, asked, "Is that the piano we're taking out?" Since it was the only piano in sight I didn't bother to answer his redundant question.

We then wheeled the piano to the doorway. I stayed topside while Dopey and Grumpy went below. Out went 850 pounds of piano with me pushing and my two not-so-friendly dwarfs catching. Once it was through the top doorway I lifted my end to manoeuvre the piano around the ninety degree bend. My job was made a lot easier because the weight of the piano was already tilting it downward. Making the turn however was anything but easy. Along with a lot of swearing coming from below and, I must admit, above as well, I could also hear the sound of drywall being ripped open. With great difficulty we made the turn and there was no turning back. Being well aware that one wrong move could possibly end up in serious injury or death we continued slowly down, one stair at a time. Miraculously, we finally made it down the stairs, out the front doorway and on to the truck. I went back upstairs to pick up the bench and piano rolls, pay the lady, apologize for the rough language and promise that I would send someone back to plaster and paint her badly damaged stairway walls. I then swore I would never buy another piano again.

Arriving back at the shop we placed the piano at the front of the store. I paid Grumpy and Dopey for their work with a little bit of a bonus to compensate for their blood loss. My wife looked at my battered and bruised body and said, "Well, at least you didn't kill yourself. I thanked her for her concern and then placed a price tag on the piano with a note stating that the purchaser would have to arrange for his or her own transportation.

The next day I was sitting in my store on my new piano bench, running my magic fingers over the keyboard while pumping away with my feet and generally having a ball. I played ragtime hits, wartime hits, love songs and the classics. A large number of piano rolls had come with the piano and I was determined to try every damn one of them. While my wife happily worked the front counter, I entertained our many customers with my amazing pumping skills. One of our customers at that time was a beautiful young girl that also happened to be a talented opera singer. Her name was Karina Gauvin. She quietly walked over to the piano, looked through the piano rolls stacked on top of the piano, selected one and asked if I would play it. I told her that my musical ability held no bounds and that I would be happy to play the classical number she selected. The fact that I couldn't even pronounce the name of the piece didn't deter me. I played and she sang. I had never heard such a beautiful voice in my life and to have this angel singing inches away from my ear was indescribable. Everyone in the store stopped what they were doing to listen.

Karina is now traveling the world and performing at all the best concert halls so I don't see much of her anymore but I'll always be indebted to her for giving this old rock and roll, Rolling Stones fan an appreciation for how truly beautiful classical music can be.

The following week I was admitted into the hospital for my hernia operation.

"THE ORIGINAL ANTIQUE LAMPS WIRING
JUST ADDS TO IT'S VALUE"

Store number 4

My experience with store number three convinced me that I could afford to open store number 4 so when a shop became available, I jumped at the opportunity. Obviously, I wasn't ready to leave the nest because number 4 was just across the street from one and two. The new store was just an antiques and collectible shop. Rent was $ 1700 a month, the highest rent I've ever had to pay so far and the new landlord was so cheap he made Ebenezer Scrooge look like a philanthropist. Commercial rents are subject to GST and PST in Canada so the rent, including taxes, was closer to $1950 per month. The second month I was there the landlord came into the shop asking me to add another two cents onto that month's rent because he had miscalculated the previous months GST and PST. I threw him a dime and told him to have a ball.

We both banked at the same location so when I told the bank teller the story of the two cents she informed me confidentially that the old skinflint had more money than God (her expression, not mine). So far I wasn't having much luck with landlords.

Running around collecting interesting antiques was much more fun than chasing down old toasters, irons, and slow cookers so I decided to sell the anchor business, close the basement shop and become a full-time antique dealer. My first shop was sold to a man from Jordan for the amazing price of ten thousand dollars. I say amazing because I had stripped it of any antiques or collectibles before selling it. I had lived off the shop for about eight years and I was still getting back ten times my initial investment.

Next door to shop four was a used book store run by Big Steve, a mountain of a man. This guy was so huge there was snow on his head in the summertime. Lying on his stomach, you could seat six on his ass. He was also one of the nicest men I have ever met and his little five foot nothing wife was precious. Her big claim to fame was attending the '69 Woodstock music festival. Steve's little business fed off of mine and I fed off of his. It was mutually beneficial and we both got along great. I remained at that location for about four years and finally fed up with a landlord that did nothing while his building was falling apart, I left for greener pastures, Store number 5.

The radio show

I was born in Ireland and came to Canada with my mother when I was two years old. My mother had a strong Irish accent and I was surrounded throughout my childhood by members of the Irish community who also spoke with strong Irish accents. I blame them all for my speech impediment. There must not be any 'THs in the Gaelic language because, to this day, I cannot pronounce TH's worth a damn. Mother comes out mudder and my three's were all trees. Not being capable of talking properly and not considering myself anything of an expert on antiques and collectibles, I knew I was the obvious choice when a local radio station approached me at store number five to do a talk show on antiques and collectibles with radio host Chuck Philips. The show was called "Ask the Expert."

I reluctantly agreed and so began my radio career. I would start the show by playing a small segment of the song "They're coming to take me away, Ha, ha, he,he, to the funny farm." After that stunning intro, I would list some of the collectibles that had recently sold at auction for, what I considered, outrageous prices. We would take a few calls from the listeners and I would try to answer their questions as honestly as possible. You would always come across the odd crackpot, like the guy who wanted to know what his 30 carat gold ring was worth. I told him he should hold on to it because it was one of a kind. Before the show I would work on pieces with Scott, the sound engineer. If we were doing a bit about movies, I would put together a series of sound clips from famous movies and then Chuck and I would discuss the values of movie posters, props, and the autographs of stars. Chuck was an articulate and refined man, so I would catch him off guard at times with subjects like collectible condoms. "Early ones come in colorful tins and many come in different colors, suitable for framing," I would announce while Chuck looked on in distress wondering what I would come up with next. When Bill Clinton was having difficulties with the U.S. House of Representitives over his sexual escapades with Monica Lewinsky, I put together a show on the value of old 45rpm vinyl records in the style of an interview with Bill, Monica and Hillary using recordings from old 45rpm records as responses. "Monica, do you have a pet name for Bill ?" I would ask and Monica would answer to the tune of "My Boy Lolipop." Listeners would be told about the original recording of the song and what the record was worth. Hillary's name for Monica was "Devil with the blue dress on" and I finished with Bill pleading "Please, don't ask about Barbara." The whole concept of my show was to instruct people on the antique and collectible market while having a good time. People reacted well to the show. I tried to warn them about the realities in the world of antiques and collectibles. Not everything that is considered valuable is valuable and many items considered of no value have a substantial value they were told. I told them about my friend whose entire house is loaded down with old cans, tin signs and primative art. Items many people would throw into the garbage or sell at a garage sale for a pittance. Most of the items in his home were valued at anywhere from hundreds to thousands and even tens of thousands of dollars. While at a garage sale, I purchased a tin of Indian gun powder for five dollars that was valued at approximately twelve hundred dollars which I sold to him for five hundred dollars. I explained to the listeners the dangers of the many fakes in the market place. Catalogues of fake depression glass, carnival glass, art glass, toys, bronzes, tiffany lamps, and every other imaginable item were printed in China and the United States. The importance of provenance for major artworks was stressed. Listeners heard about another acquaintance of mine who had purchased a major work of art and had already spent well over twenty thousand dollars trying to establish its credentials. Knowing in your heart that a painting is authentic is not enough. You have to be able to convince your staunchest critic. He was running into the age-old problem of half the experts claiming it a fake and the other half verifying its authenticity.

My show ran for a number of years but then the station turned to an all news format and that was that.

Gone but Not Forgotten

While in the process of organizing an estate sale you learn a lot about the recently departed. The books and magazines they read, the games they played, the photographs they kept and the mementoes they cherished all tell a story. You can also learn about their still lingering family and friends.

Some of the personality traits I have observed over the years were admirable and some were disturbing. I remember one substantial estate where a father died leaving no will or named executor resulting in a long legal battle between his two sons over the split of his cash and investments, home and contents. From the seniors' residence in which she was incarcerated, the mother's poor health and slightly diminished mental state left her no option but to look sadly on as her family was torn apart and her husband's estate dwindled away in legal fees. The only thing the brothers finally achieved was the death of their mother and total alienation from each other and the rest of the family.

After witnessing that particular fiasco, I immediately went out and had a detailed will made up with an executor named. When I die, my kids will have nobody to blame but me for the distribution of my remaining assets and I will be beyond caring. After all, what can they do? Kill me?

Some kids like to get the jump on estate asset distribution. An older client of mine accidentally discovered that her nieces and nephews were splitting up her estate while she was still very much alive and kicking. She was sitting in her favourite Victorian chair one day enjoying good health and a cookie when the cookie dropped out of her hand and rolled under a coffee table. Bending to pick it up, she noticed a piece of paper stapled to the bottom of the table. Written on the paper was the name of one of her nieces. The discovery started her on a search of the many other household assets belonging to her. Hidden under clocks, inside silver cases, and behind paintings she discovered more pieces of paper bearing the names of nieces and nephews. She promptly removed all the name designations, burned them in her fireplace and scheduled an appointment with her notary. A new will was made out leaving all her assets to a charitable foundation.

Eventually, with every estate an unlucky family member is delegated the difficult task of clearing out the contents of the home. This individual is often the last to step forward and the first to be criticized for the way they handled the job nobody wanted. It's always difficult clearing out the home of a beloved family member or friend. Most items usually carry more of an emotional value than a monetary one and you are ultimately facing a deadline. Hopefully, the job isn't made more difficult by feuding family members or friends making real, imagined or fictional claims on the most cherished and valuable items in the estate.

When faced with the task of clearing an estate, you have various options.

1- Hold an estate sale yourself

2- Auction off the contents of the home

3- Bring in professional estate liquidators and evaluators

4- Distribute the assets among the family and friends and give what remains to charity

Last, but not least, is the option of holding on to everything, thereby turning your home into a long-range storage facility filled with boxes that will never be opened and furniture that will never be used. Or, pay out monthly fees to a storage company where the total cost of storage could eventually exceed the total value of the goods stored.

You can put a price on sentiment and the price is calculated in terms of a cluttered home or climbing storage costs.

We sometimes forget that the most valuable and long-lasting things left behind are the memories of loving and happy times shared together which take up space in our hearts, not our homes, and cost nothing to store.

A few small tips when having an estate sale

1- You should always check to see if there was anything held in storage (review cash and bank transactions to see if there were any storage charges). When clearing out a condo or an apartment, find out if there was a locker assigned to the unit.

2- Before opening up the home to the public it is always advisable to make sure that there is nothing embarrassing or personal lying around. Clearing out the home of a single man I once found four dildos hidden in his bedroom closet. I would have preferred it if he had collected stamps.

3- Look out for hidden money. In one home, I found over twenty thousand dollars hidden in books, under drawers,

behind pictures and in every other possible hiding place imaginable around the house. The trustees were very happy with the discovery and gave me a great big thank you. No reward, just a thank you. I was so moved by their gracious thank you that I was compelled to give them a thank you gesture in return.

4- Try to have someone knowledgeable look over the estate before holding the sale. You don't want to sell valuable items at dollar store prices.

Store number five

Five was the largest store I had rented to date. It was approximately three thousand square feet with a five hundred square foot loading dock in the back and another three thousand square feet of basement space. My old customers at first questioned my ability to fill the store. Then, within three months, they expressed their concern that the store wasn't big enough. A section of the store was devoted to second-hand clothing. This was a new venture for me, and it turned out to be a profitable one. Every estate sale had clothing for sale at a cheap price and, in the wealthy areas of town, the clothing often had designer labels attached. There was also an amazing market in retro clothing. There was a demand for everything such as Nehru jackets, bell bottom jeans, tie dyes, mini skirts, Pillbox hats and Go-Go boots. Then, there was the vintage market with the Victorian and flapper dresses and Zoot suits.

Baby clothing was another market. People would think nothing of paying high prices for baby outfits a child would quickly grow out of and then sell those outfits for pocket change at a garage sale. I also opened a second hand book section that sold books, old vinyl records, VHS movies (DVDs weren't available at the time) and taped music. The mark-up on these items was amazing.

The balance of my store was devoted to second-hand furniture, decorative items and antiques. Business was going great with a few screw-ups along the way. There was the drunk that came into the store, staggered into an area closed to the public and fell down a flight of stairs breaking his arm. Just my luck, the inebriated man's wife was a lawyer and I ended up with a lawsuit on my hands. There was the time my handyman decided to repair my outside electrical sign without first turning off the power and ended lit up like a stripper at a near-sighted men's convention.

My biggest mistake in store number five was only signing a two year lease. When the landlord saw how successful my business was, he decided to cash in on my success and raised the rent substantially.

I told him to do something that was virtually and physically impossible, considering the size of the store, and went on to store number six.

Gypsy

When you have a wife like mine it's one animal rescue after another. One day I arrived at the store just to be sent out again on an animal rescue mission. The hairdresser half a block away had called to tell Marilyn all about a sick tabby cat that was lying outside her door. My instructions were to go over, check out the cat and if necessary, bring it to a vet. Being an obedient yet slightly exasperated husband I did what I was told and went out the door mumbling, "If your hairdresser is so damned concerned, why doesn't *she* do something about it?"

Having been sent on rescue missions before and having the scars to prove it, I approached the cat very carefully. She was lying down quietly so I eventually threw caution to the wind, picked her up and checked her over. She allowed herself to be subjected to my thorough inspection without once expressing any displeasure. She was malnourished and had a badly infected injury on her back. There go the day's profits, I thought, as I carried her carefully to my truck and headed out to our local vet. After a complete check-up, he cleaned and closed the wound, prescribed antibiotics and suggested I have her neutered when she was feeling better and put on a little weight. Throughout this ordeal, the cat never once voiced the slightest complaint. Agreeing to return to have the stitches removed, I headed back to the store with my new-found friend sitting peacefully on the seat beside me. When Marilyn saw the cat, it was love at first sight. She decided this little character had gone through enough misery in her life and things were about to change. Since we already had an outlaw cat with a nasty disposition, ironically named Cuddles, at home she decided it would be wiser to give our new friend the honorary title of Store Cat. My pleas of "Honey, if she bites one of our customers we could be sued and there are hundreds of items around here she can break. Let's think about this" were ignored.

"Look at her" she answered "She's so gentle she wouldn't hurt a mouse. We'll call her Gypsy since she was found in the street."

Over the next two weeks, Gypsy got stronger as the wound healed and she began to put on weight. She developed a real appreciation for fine antiques and would curl up in each newly acquired antique chair. She always let the customers pet and kiss her without once complaining. If Marilyn and I were busy at the counter she would come over, jump up and rub her back against our arms seeking attention. One day a woman came in claiming that Gypsy belonged to her, and she wanted her back. "Gypsy was near death when we found her," she was told, "If you want her back, cough up the vet bills." I must admit with some guilt that I highly exaggerated the cost of her treatment. That's the last we saw of the lady.

Gypsy turned out to be the best sales clerk I ever had. She sold every chair and loveseat she slept on. Customers would visit the shop just to see her. In the ten years we had her she never bit a customer, never hissed at anyone, never broke a dish as she jumped from table to table, and never left the shop. In summer, our front and back doors were always open and although she would walk to the door and look out, she never walked out. Gypsy knew where she was loved.

When she eventually got old and sickly we called the vet asking him to come to the store and put her gently asleep on the newly acquired antique chair she now rested on.

There were a lot of tears shed throughout the neighbourhood that week.

The Strangest Dream

After awaking one morning I immediately started moving my hands and feet and then called out my name in a loud clear voice. Strange behavior, one might think, but considering the nightmare I had just had, I didn't consider it strange at all.

In my dream I was talking on one of my favorite subjects to a classroom full of students. The subject was antiques and collectibles. Spread out near the door of the classroom were old swords, medals, firearms, antique carpenter's tools, dishes, photographs and an antique chest. As I started speaking, one of the students in the back of the classroom yelled out, "Speak up, we can't hear you in the back."

Straining to raise my voice and continue with my talk, I suddenly realized I was losing my power of speech. My voice was getting weaker and slower and I began fighting to get each word out. Believing in the importance of my message, I struggled on, much to the consternation of the students in the room.

With my hands on the top of an old 18th century Quebec pine trunk I struggled to say, "Like us, antiques have a body, a soul and hold precious memories. Unlike us they do not have the power of speech or the power to record those memories. The items I have brought to you today have lived through the Indian wars, civil wars, wars of independence and two major world wars. They have witnessed the industrial revolution, the roaring twenties, the great depression, the sexual revolution of the sixties and the coming of the Beatles and the death of Elvis Presley."

My voice weakened and fighting this weakness I began to walk around the classroom and noticed looks of concern on the faces of the students, many I now recognized as old friends.

Michael's ever cheerful smile was fading, Frank's usual bon vivant expression was wilting and Martin looked like he was ready to bolt from the room and call 911.

Still struggling but determined to defeat whatever it was that was attacking my body, I told the room, "You have all been given a precious gift and that gift is the ability to record and preserve history. You should never take that gift lightly. Keeping a diary, writing small pieces for your local papers, using the social media (carefully), capturing moments with new and improved digitalized cameras and keeping accurate records help preserve the history of your family, your friendships and your community."

As I struggled to get out the next word, tears rolled down my cheeks. I apologized to the class for my inappropriate behavior and informed them that I would unfortunately have to cut short my talk. I left the room realizing I was suffering from a stroke and would need immediate medical assistance. The crazy thing was that knowing I could be dead at any moment, my main concern was how I would get all my antique samples back into my truck and transport them safely back to the store.

After awaking from this disturbing dream I came to a number of realizations, the first of which was the fact that material possessions take on way too much importance in this delicate life we live. The second was how one small quirk of fate can lead to major changes in our lives, our lifestyles and how we relate to others and how others relate to us. No one is immune to these quirks of fate, not the poor, nor the middle class, not the rich nor the pretentious. All our bodies and all our possessions will eventually end up as dust, ash or land fill. Our precious souls, however, will live on and each and every act of kindness will live on in the hearts of those we loved, knew, or simply bumped into when they were hurting, vulnerable or in need of help, a kind word or a smile.

I came to the realization that my dream was, in fact, a call to reality...a call to perhaps reevaluate my lifestyle, my priorities, and myself. Am I one of the antiques whose history I was so desperately trying to preserve?

When writing this small piece I made a few strange typographical errors making me wonder if it was all just a dream.

The game

One night at about two o'clock in the morning, I woke up with this crazy idea in my head that wouldn't go away. Tossing and turning I tried to get back to sleep but it was impossible so I decided to get up, start up my computer and work on polishing up my dream project. When Marilyn woke up at eight in the morning, I was still on the computer working away. The blueprint for what I considered the greatest game since Monopoly and Trivial Pursuit was now on my computer and it took another two years to finalzse it. The entire concept of the game was to accomplish the same goal as my radio show, to educate and entertain on the subject of antiques and collectibles. The game had to be designed so that even those with no interest in the subject would be entertained and enlightened. I accomplished my goal and then left it on the drawing board. There were a lot of sharks out there; I knew because I had come across many of them. My fear was a big game company would steal my design and I would be left with nothing to show for my work while they took the credit and got rich. This had happened to me once before. Once bitten, twice shy.

The concept of the game was simple; you start with a set amount of money and travel around a board answering questions about antiques and collectibles and collecting as much money and valuables as you can on the way around. The man or woman with the most cash and valuables at the end of the game wins the title of North American Antique Expert. My questions were designed so that everyone could play, even antique ignoramuses.

Questions such as:

What do we mean when we say that a young German girl blew Kugels for Christmas?

A- Glass blowing of traditional German Holiday drinking glasses
B- Glass blowing of ornaments to decorate the house and tree with at Christmas
C-A great Christmas gift for Hans Kugel
ANSWER: B
(with an honorable mention to anyone who chose C)

AND

True or False
The popular musical group, The Beatles, marketed a product called
RINGO BUBBLE BATH
The product was advertised by the slogan
LEAVE A RINGO AROUND YOUR TUB
ANSWER: FALSE
The product was real - the slogan is just the creation from the warped mind of the game designer.
Or, more serious questions
On December 8, 1980 Mark David Chapman fired four shots that killed John Lennon.
Which item belonging to Mark Chapman was reportedly sold at auction for $400,000?
Left unclaimed and then, later, resold at auction for $150,000
A-The book he was holding, J.D. Salinger's "Catcher in the Rye"
B-An autographed copy of the Double Fantasy Album
C-the 38 revolver used to kill John

ANSWER B

The world we live in was made richer by John Lennon's birth and poorer by his death. Collecting memorabilia associated with his killer might prove profitable, but could be considered ethically questionable

After creating about one thousand questions and answers, I then attacked the other cards. There were six main ways to collect money and valuables in this game. One way was to become an auctioneer and collect a commission on every item sold, another was to circle the board as fast as possible collecting money for every full circle. You could also make money with smart purchases at flea markets, garage sales and auctions. The last method is by drawing Agony and Ecstasy cards.

There were rather simple rules to accomplish these goals.

Samples of the cards are:

AUCTION CARDS

The man or woman landing on "auction house" becomes the auctioneer and everyone around the table can bid on the item described on the top auction house card.

The reverse side of the card shows a value given to this item based on actual recorded auction results. These values are kept hidden from everyone during the auction and revealed only to the purchaser after the auction is over.

AUCTION HOUSE

Early 20th century charger
'Bizarre by Clarice Cliff'

Opening bid
$1000

FLEA MARKET CARD

FLEA MARKET

ANTIQUE
Victorian Paper Mache Ecritoire
Writers's Lap Desk

Price $500

When you land on "flea market" you have the option to buy, at the stated price, the item shown on the top flea market card. If you don't wish to purchase the item you can pass on your option to the next player on your left. He,in turn, can buy the item or pass on the option to the next player on his left. If all the players around the table reject the item, the card goes to the bottom of the deck.

The flip side of this card shows the actual value of the item.

GARAGE SALE CARDS

GARAGE SALE

Early 20th century British candy tin
Good condition
11 inches high

Price $100

When a player lands on the "garage sale" square, he or she has the option to pick one of the top three cards on the "garage sale" deck. Once the choice is made they pay the banker and check the back of the chosen card to see if their pick was a wise or foolish one.

At a realized value of five hundred dollars, this would be a very wise choice indeed.

AGONY AND ECSTACY CARDS

These cards have cartoons that award or penalize you based on your card selection.

The Agony & the Ecstacy

The beauty of the game is that it was designed to teach as well as entertain. All values stated are based on values realized in the real world so that players can learn valuable lessons that could result in making real money in that real world.

THE ANTIQUES & COLLECTIBLES GAME

One day a friend of mine came up to me and told me that someone had put out a game on antiques and collectibles. My heart came to a sudden stop. I decided to get a copy of the newly-discovered game and compare it to mine and was glad to discover that the similarities were on subject matter only.

Testing had to be done so I arranged to have a few friends over, including one that hated board games, to check out my game against the competition. We played the published game for 5 minutes and everyone agreed enough was enough.

My game came out next and we played for over two hours before calling it quits.
The friend who hated board games wanted to know when we could play again..
Creating this game made me realize I just had way too much time on my hands.

Years after developing the game, I finally worked up the nerve to approach a toy maker with my concept. He told me that it was interesting but the days of board games were over and the new generation of kids wanted computer action games only.

I sadly put it back on the shelf.

Prototype of game board

My brother

I have spent decades searching peoples' attics, basements, garages, and crawl spaces. I have fought my way through cluttered houses with plaster falling from the ceiling, leaking, damp and mouldy basements, and rodent-infested attics and never experienced any serious health problems. My brother breaks his ankle on New Year's Eve, ends up in a hospital room where he comes into contact with c.difficile and dies within six months.

The sad irony is that all those bacteria-saturated surroundings didn't give me as much as a sniffle and a hospital, that is supposed to guarantee a healthy environment, killed my brother.

At his funeral, I gave this eulogy that I include here because it applies to many other brothers, sisters, mothers, fathers, sons and daughters out there.

EULOGY FOR A BROTHER

There are two quotations I'd like to share. One is from a book by Harper Lee about racism, intolerance, and injustice. The second quote is from an unknown source.

THE FIRST QUOTE IS

"Remember IT'S A SIN TO KILL A MOCKINGBIRD "*

That was the first time I ever heard Atticus say it was a sin to do something, and I asked Miss Maudie about it. "Your Father's right" she said," mockingbirds don't do one thing but make music for us to enjoy... but sing their hearts out for us. That's why it's a sin to kill a mockingbird."

AND THE OTHER IS

LOVE NEVER DIES A NATURAL DEATH. IT DIES BECAUSE
WE DON'T KNOW HOW TO REPLENISH IT'S SOURCE. IT
DIES OF BLINDNESS AND ERRORS AND BETRAYALS

My brother was admitted with a broken ankle to the hospital
on New Year's Eve, December 31, 2002.

My brother died Saturday June 14, 2003 after spending 6
months in that hospital and undergoing two operations on his
ankle, five major operations on his stomach, one major
operation on his throat, many minor operations and more x-
rays that any man or woman should ever have to endure in a
lifetime. During this time, he was given barely anything to eat
and little to drink. For fourteen days he was tied hand and foot
to his bed, unable to turn, unable to get comfortable, unable
to clear his throat and suffering from severe stomach disorders.

*Months ago, a doctor took my mother aside and told her that, "we're
very sorry but your son died of a heart attack."*

*Minutes later that statement was corrected to, "Well, it seems he
didn't die but his heart stopped for a long period of time and you
can expect serious brain damage."*

*Within two days my brother was asking if I had completed his
income tax return and wondering if he should give me his power of
attorney so that I could handle his financial affairs. Some people
might consider the fact that he wanted me to have his power of
attorney an indication of serious brain damage but I can assure you
that his brain was operating just fine.*

*When you asked my brother how he was feeling, he usually said,
"Oh not bad."*

He seldom complained and was always considerate of his family and the nursing staff.

He never accused anyone, not the doctors, or the nurses, of being out to kill him.

This man my brother, while being subjected to all manner of torture, discomfort and indignities over six months in the hospital never once made any wild accusations.

This man, my brother diagnosed and medicated for forty years as a paranoid schizophrenic accepted what was happening to him without anger or accusations.

We were informed that during this six month stay at the hospital, he was given few of his regular psychiatric medications.

We put our faith in the medical professional in the strong belief that they have the training, the education and the compassion, therefore they know best.

They betrayed us.

It's a sin to kill a mockingbird because they are defenseless, fragile and do nothing but bring beauty into this world.

My brother was fragile, defenseless. He touched many people with his kindness, his compassion and his generosity. He had little but what he had, he shared.

There were some wonderful nurses and doctors at that hospital and there were some less than wonderful practitioners of the medical profession at that hospital. To those that fit the second category, I say I feel sorry for you

You have killed a mockingbird and you will have to live with that sin for the rest of your lives.

A doctor told my other brother Kevin that everybody dies and "after all, your brother is an older man."

It's amazing how sixty-two might seem old when you're in your thirties and looking at someone else's life. However when looking at your own life and the lives of your children and loved ones, sixty-two doesn't seem that old at all.

This same doctor said, "Well, he didn't have a great quality of life before and if he survives, that quality of life would be greatly diminished."

What did this pompous ass know about my brother's quality of life? My brother knew of its quality because he fought so hard to hold on to it. He didn't measure the quality of a person's life by the size of his home, or the car in his driveway, or the number of gold and platinum cards he had in his wallet.

He measured the quality of his life by the love of his family and friends. He measured the quality of his life by the number of people he could help and touch in a positive way every day of that life.

LOVE NEVER DIES A NATURAL DEATH. IT DIES BECAUSE WE DON'T KNOW HOW TO REPLENISH ITS SOURCE. IT DIES OF BLINDNESS AND ERRORS AND BETRAYALS.

According to reported research studies, there are approximately 195,000 deaths a year in America due to medical error.

Twenty-four-thousand such deaths a year were reported in Canada.

My brother was crucified in that hospital.

Instead of a cross, he was bound to a bed and instead of a hammer, nails and a spear, they used the weapons of indifference, ignorance, selfishness and greed.

The ignorance and indifference of the doctor who sees no further than the scribbling of Paranoia Schizophrenic on a medical chart.

The greed and selfishness of every politician that was so busy filling his pockets and the pockets of his friends and supporters that he neglected to leave enough funds to support our medical system.

My brother was crucified in a hospital bed for six months and his loving mother was at the foot of that bed doing all she could to make him more comfortable.

This world of ours grows poorer every time a good man or women dies.

The world is poorer today.

My brother died.

* Published by Time Warner

Store number six

With the exception of a couple of floods and a minor fire, things went pretty well at store number six until I decided that working six days a week, twelve hours a day and fighting traffic to and from home was not for me.

Off to the country we went.

A NEW LIFE IN A SMALL TOWN

Eleven years ago my wife, Marilyn, and I decided it was time to sell our beautiful but quaint home in Beaconsfield and move to the country. Our home had a wonderful 14,000 square foot backyard overlooking a major highway and the rail lines. After 20 years of being serenaded nightly by 16 wheelers and freight trains, we figured it was time to move on.

We contacted a real estate agent and told him our requirements - stipulating that if he showed us any properties within a 20-mile radius of a train station or major highway we would personally see to it that he sang soprano for the rest of his life. After showing us a number of properties that were all rejected for one valid reason or another, he decided, at great personal risk, to show us a newly-listed property in the small town of Hudson that was close to, but not on top of, the railway tracks. Marilyn fell in love with the house and property and I, with considerable prompting, made an offer that could be, but wasn't, refused. That real estate agent is now available as lead female soprano to any opera production.

So, as the song goes, we loaded up our truck with all the antiques and collectibles we had collected over the years and moved on to Hudson. Our first month in a small town was somewhat of a surreal experience. We discovered that it's not easy getting to sleep without trains, sixteen wheelers, or racing cars lulling you off to quiet bliss. We also discovered that country air can be highly invigorating. Marilyn and I were flabbergasted when all our neighbours started dropping by to introduce themselves and welcome us to the community. I told Marilyn that a mutual love of antiques has finally resulted in time-travelling to the way things used to be before the advent of big city life, computers and satellite TV. Our next door neighbour Kathy invited us to her annual wine and cheese party welcoming new arrivals to the neighbourhood. I remember showing up at the party with my bottle of Jameson's Irish whiskey. Being Irish, I mistakenly assumed that when she said wine, as in Wine and Cheese Party, she was only speaking figuratively. I felt slightly out of place until my new neighbour Derek, a retired schoolteacher, yelled out to my other new neighbour Vladimir, a urologist, "Hey Vladimir, I hope you washed your hands before you handled that cheese." Vladimir just smiled and I instantly felt at home. By the end of the evening, and with the help of my new friends, the bottle of Jamison's was empty and I had scheduled an early morning rendezvous with Derek and his lovely wife Joy. They were going to show us some of the Hudson hiking paths. True to their word, Derek and Joy were outside our door in the morning, ready to go. We discovered wonderful trails that day and from that day on it was discovery after discovery. We discovered Sandy Beach, the Wharf, the Village Theatre, Finnegan's Market, Pine Lake, Vivery Creek, and many amazing restaurants and shops. We discovered that, if you're into preserving wildlife, you could volunteer at the Nichoir a wild bird clinic and conservatory, or hand out vitamin pills at the Chateau du Lac, the local drinking establishment.

My neighbour Kathy noticed that I was somewhat pudgy so she suggested that I go with her to the morning exercise workout at St. James church. I reluctantly agreed - but only on the condition that we start off slow with the senior class. After a ninety-year-old woman blew by me on the running track, I quit. My ego couldn't take the punishment.

My exercise now consists of flying around the Como Golf Club on a golf cart, trying desperately to put a little white ball into a small cup.

I found out that there's a lot to do in a small town if you want to get involved. There's the local Legion, the curling clubs, the golf clubs, fishing off the wharf or at Pine Lake, the exercise or kick boxing classes, the theatre group, Greenwood, the Historical Society and the Garden Club. The list goes on and on.

In the winter time, you have the Santa Claus parade, the Winter Carnival, the Festival of Lights, Snow Golf and A Greenwood Christmas.

I now live in a small town with a small town attitude - and I say that with the utmost pride.

If being small town means knowing and helping your neighbours, then I want to be small town. If being small town means respecting and helping out your community, then I want to be small town. If being small town means not being able to shop at your local market without stopping to talk with the many neighbours you meet, then I'm proud to say I'm from a small town.

One year after moving to Hudson, Marilyn said, "Honey, lets close our shop in the City and open up here." I listened to her and moved my shop from the big city to the small town of Hudson and my income dropped lower than George Bush Junior's IQ - but my quality of life went up tenfold, so I guess it was a good move. I might change my mind if I hear the local minister preaching, "Yes, we *can* take it with us." For now, I'll just go on sleeping at night to the sounds of silence and waking each morning to the songs of the birds and the barking of my dogs.

Just another day in a small town.

eBay

E-Bay went public on September 21, 1998 and their target share price of $18 went to $53.50 on the first day of trading and I didn't invest. What a mistake! I knew it was a great idea that was bound to succeed. After all, I had been in the antiques and collectibles business for 16 years by then and I knew it's potential. Being computer illiterate didn't help and when all my friends were raking it in during the early days of eBay, I just continued on my merry way dealing with customers over the counter and enjoying my life. "This E-Bay thing is going to turn around and bite you in the ass one day" I would say and they all laughed saying "Frank's paranoia was kicking in again."

Maybe I was being paranoid or maybe I wasn't. All I know is that the competition at garage sales went up drastically and it seemed that everyone with access to a computer was now a competitor. In the past, people sold their antiques locally in a garage sale or to a dealer but now they had a new world-wide option and if they didn't know how to take advantage of it, they had a son, daughter, niece or nephew who did. Millions of items were being sold on eBay and prices began to drop on some items and go crazy on others. Where we used to ask "What does the price guide list the value at?" we were now saying, "What does it sell on eBay for?" Many collectors were checking the world-wide market for that old lighter or fountain pen rather than rummaging through every antique store in town.

The business had changed. Some believed it changed for the better and some believed for the worse. All I knew for sure was that our private club was no longer private and we could either climb on for the ride or be left behind.

Auctions

Going to country auctions is a great way of collecting interesting and often inexpensive antiques. The rule often applies that the more remote the auction, the better the bargain. Sometimes I have to smile when I hear the values given to antiques on one of the many antique shows that grace the airwaves. Those values are often based on the auction values realized at some of the more prominent auction houses and those values are not cast in steel. Prices have varied substantially from one auction house to another just as prices vary from store to store. To get the best price for an item, there has to be a lot of interest generated on that item and bidders have to be highly competitive. Two bidders who refuse to cry uncle will put a smile on any auctioneer's and seller's face. As with everything else, there are good and bad auctioneers and you have to be very careful who you leave your stock with. Over my many years in business, I have heard more than a few sad tales about people who left items on consignment with antique shops and auctioneers just to discover that the goods and the consignee have vanished. When you think of it, it's a hell of a scam. They rent a store or warehouse maybe even negotiating a month or two free rent and then advertise that they take things on consignment. After running the place for a few months and filling it with interesting collectibles, they suddenly disappear taking all the goods and money with them. Moving to another town, they start all over again under a different name. The police have no interest in the matter because the theft of the goods is considered a civil, not a criminal matter because the client willingly parted with the goods under contract. The clients' choices are to either incur heavy legal cost trying to recover their money and goods under breach of contract or lick their wounds and walk away. Most people just walk away.

There are many tricks one has to watch out for in buying at auction from questionable auctioneers. Some of these tricks are ethically wrong and some can be considered ethically questionable or just good business. The decision is ours to make.

A) Always attend the preview. Flaws on items are not always well described or sometimes not described at all by an auctioneer. If you purchase an item and find it badly flawed, your legal options will be limited if that item was available for preview.

B) Watch out for wording that can be misleading.

(In the style of Louis XV) does not mean it is a period piece. It could have been made last week.

(Pine finish) does not mean it is made of pine. The piece could be made of cheap pressboard finished with a pine veneer.

(Attributed to) Attributed to Pablo Picasso does not necessarily mean it was painted by Picasso. It could have been painted by Diego Garcia, the house painter from down the block.

C) Ghost bidders or plants can be used by some auctioneers to help drive up prices and interest. Some justification might arguably be considered if the item in question has a reserved price and the auctioneer's friendly ghost stops bidding just before the set reserve.

There is no justification whatsoever if that ghost bids on unreserved items or continues bidding after the reserve price is met.

D) When bidding, always consider the total cost including tax and auctioneer's premium.

E) Beware when an auctioneer uses a previous auction result to justify his evaluation of the piece for sale. Caspar the friendly ghost, might have been the last buyer.

F) Read the auction contract to be aware of all costs and periods of payment. Auctioneers can hold back funds until they're certain all checks and Interact transactions have cleared and there was no recourse claimed by the buyer.

Some auctioneers will have weekly auctions that draw bargain hunters and small dealers, monthly, bi-monthly or yearly specialized catalogued auctions drawing big shots with the deep pockets. There are often additional charges associated with the catalogued auction.

When you set a reserved price (the minimum allowable price of the piece) there is often a cost associated with it. I have seen cases where people were required to pay an auctioneer to recover their own stock because some of their goods did not reach the reserve price and the money due to the auctioneer was greater than the money collected by the auctioneer.

G) Attend the auction to insure that the auctioneer doesn't use the quick hammer (knocking an item down as sold without allowing or ignoring further bidding). This is done by auctioneers wishing to buy the item for themselves or granting a favor to a friend.

While at the auction, keep a record of what your items sold for and to which paddle numbers just in case the auctioneer comes up with a different amount.

There are many fine auctioneers and fine antique dealers out there but a bit of caution is always recommended.

"DAMN, IT STILL WORKS!"

The corruption of power

In a business like mine you go on many house calls and no two are alike. Some calls are amusing, some annoying and some are sad. An elderly lady called me to her home because she said, "I've lost my house and have to move to a seniors' residence." I went over to see her and after a few opening pleasantries asked what happened to change her fortunes. She told me she placed all her savings in the hands of a Mr. Earl Jones and that Jones had recently been arrested for running a Ponzi scheme and her money was gone. She had mortgaged her home after checking with Jones about a world tour she wanted to go on with some friends. "He convinced me not to touch my savings," she said, "He claimed they were making great returns and I should take out another mortgage on my home instead at the low mortgage rates available." She listened to him and lost everything.

British historian Lord Acton, in a letter he wrote in 1887, said: "Power tends to corrupt; absolute power corrupts absolutely." This is not an absolute, as there are no absolutes in this world of ours except death and taxation, but the quotation applies as much today as it did then. We see exceptions to this rule in men like Sir Frederick Banting, who sold his car to finance his research and then sold the rights to his insulin discovery for $1 so that everyone could afford the medication and in men like General Romeo Dallaire who tried to stop the genocide in Rwanda.

At the other end of the spectrum, there are men like Earl Jones, Bernard Madoff (charged with securities fraud), Jeffery Skillings (of Enron, sentenced to 24 years for insider trading and fraud), and Bernard Ebber's (of Worldcom, serving a 25 year sentence for accounting fraud). These men, and many others like them, used their power and position to manipulate the system for gain and fame. Because of their actions, seniors like the woman I visited were seeing their pensions reduced radically, losing their homes, businesses and jobs. Families are broken apart and people have died, either directly or indirectly, because of the actions of the greedy few. Even the most unscrupulous antique dealers I know come out as saints compared to some of those men.

I ask myself how a man becomes a monster. Is the white collar monster any more humane than the black shirt monster? The question brings to mind an incident from my younger days when I was working in a management position for Northern Electric. I had a meeting at the head office on Dorchester Street. It was a cold and snowy winter day and being young, full of energy and dressed in my finest suit and winter coat, I decided to walk to my destination. Taking a shortcut through a laneway I noticed a man lying on the ground. I ran to his aid, thinking he might have suffered a stroke or heart attack. Bending down to check him out I discovered that the man was totally drunk, unable to stand, had urinated in his pants and had vomited all over his clothing. I left him there, within half a block from a homeless shelter, and rushed on to my meeting. I have no knowledge of what eventually happened to that man and I have always regretted the decision I made that day. I failed to see the man; I only saw his sorry condition. I dehumanized him and, once dehumanized, he was easy to ignore. My fancy coat, suit and job took priority over that poor man's life. If tested again, I hope I will not fail so miserably.

People in power are tested constantly and many in finance, politics and other positions of trust as well as some antique dealers have put their fancy coats, suits and lifestyle first. They just close their eyes and continue business as usual. They don't see the victim, only the benefits derived from their actions. Their philosophy is that profit comes first and all other considerations are secondary. Many didn't even believe they were doing anything seriously wrong; it was just good business.

There's a biblical saying, "The meek shall inherit the earth."

Let's hope it won't be after the arrogant are finished with it.

'IT'S OLD, CRACKED AND DOESN'T HOLD WATER ... JUST LIKE ME!'

Trash or Treasure

The seasoned professionals in the antique and collectible world already know the tricks of the trade on how to separate trash from treasure. The novice, however, might not. It's impossible to go into full details on every aspect of every field because it is much too large but sometimes a small sample can stimulate the appetite and stop someone from making a costly mistake.

PAINTINGS

Many people can't differentiate between an original and a print. Beautifully framed prints on canvas arrive daily from China where the population is big and the hourly wage small. These prints often have brush strokes applied to give them the look and feel of original oil. Some of these prints are planted at estate sales to sucker the unsuspecting client.

Before buying, you should always study a painting closely. Is the frame antique or does it only look antique? Some frames are worth more than the painting but beware the dealer that tries to purchase your priceless work of art by telling you, "I only want it for the frame."

Does the back of the canvas show age and how is the canvas stretched in the old or new style? Watch out for artificial aging. One dealer I knew would stain the back of his canvases with tea bags to give them an older look.

Is it a print or a water color? Many original water colors are sold as prints at garage and estate sales. The picture should be checked with a high powered magnifying lens. You can usually identify a print by the series of microscopic dots that make up the picture.

Is it a signed and numbered print or an artist's proof? Many artists make a limited edition of prints (1/50 one of fifty or 500/3000 five hundred of three thousand) and sign and number each one giving them additional value. An artist proof is a signed print by the artist with the letters AP indicating that this was the original print approved by the artist prior to printing the run.

There are also woodcuts, etchings, lithographs, engravings, silk screens, clip art, digital art and computer-generated art all adding to the confusion.

A common error I have noted in the world of art pertains to bronze sculptures. People often mistake the cheaper bronze coloured metal spelter (mostly zinc) for true bronze (mostly copper). Spelter is much lighter and if scratched the base of a spelter piece will show a silver scratch When purchasing a bronze, I always check out the quality of the workmanship and look to see if it has a foundry mark. Most bronzes are also stamped with the artist's signature. There are many inexpensive mass produced bronzes hitting the market place and copies of famous artists like Frederic Remington can be found everywhere.

Finding a great work of art is exciting but does not always lead to riches. Fakes exist, some dating back to the time of the original. Therefore, professional art dealers often require the provenance (proven history) of the piece. The science of establishing the authenticity of a work of art can be expensive and may not always end in a satisfactory conclusion. If you can find a name on the painting you are selling it might be wise to check out the artist on the internet before selling. Two sites I use are findartinfo.com and artprice.com

RUGS

I recently went to a garage sale and witnessed a beautiful hand made Persian rug being sold for fifty dollars. The seller believed it to be a cheap machine made rug of no true value.

You should always check the back of a rug when buying or selling. Are the knots close tight knots? Is there a slight irregularity to the weave? Do the colors on the back match the front? Is the rug vegetable dyed? An answer of *yes* to all of these questions would indicate that you probably have a hand made rug and further research is necessary before disposing of it.

The value of oriental rugs can be anywhere from a few hundred dollars to tens of thousands of dollars depending on the age, materials, design, condition, country of origin and history.

CHINA, PORCELAIN AND POTTERY

The first thing you should do when selling your grandmother's old vase is to check the markings on the bottom.

If the vase has England stamped on its bottom (I have Ireland tattooed on mine) then it was probably made after 1891 when the US McKinley Tariff Act made it compulsory for companies to indicate the country of origin on all wares. If it states, Made in England, it was probably made after 1914. If it states dishwasher safe we can rule out any real antique value but collector value is still a possibility.

Then check to see if there is a company name indicated on the bottom. Run that name through the internet. There are many famous names that demand high prices and sometimes a five minute internet search can put a smile on your face from ear to ear.

Very early porcelain and pottery might only show a series of dots, or an anchor, crossed swords, or arrow. These symbols might represent the important factories of Minton, Chelsea, Meissen or Bow and the age of the piece. I say might because many of these symbols have been copied by others. Books on porcelain and pottery marks can often be found at your local bookstore, library, or over the internet (Amazon & Booksellers.com)

ADVERTISING MEMORABILIA

I'll never forget the time I arrived at a south shore home and was directed into an empty basement by the eighty-five year old woman in charge. She was cleaning out her older brother's home and found an old rusty sword that someone suggested might have some value. She wanted to show me it to me. I told her that due to its condition, lack of real age and uniqueness the sword had little value. I asked her what happened to the rest of the items that must have been in the basement.

"My brother was a pack rat" she said, "he had this basement filled with old Coca Cola advertising signs. It took me forever to clear it out."

"Please, don't tell me you threw them out" I cried.

"Why yes, the signs and an old Lionel electric train set he had as a child, it hadn't worked for years" she replied.

Her first statement knocked me down and her second put the boots to me.

A good friend of mine makes a very good living just dealing with old advertising memorabilia. The general rule of thumb is age, rarity, condition and artistic merit all add to value. If it's a cross collectible (attractive to two different kinds of collector) the value goes up.

Tins with early golfers, baseball players, trains, ships and early aviation will normally demand higher values.

Items that accurately, stylistically or whimsically reflect an era of time can have a substantial value.

JEWELRY

Some early designer jewelry can demand higher prices than jewelry made of silver and gold so it's always advisable to check it out before you chuck it out. After all my years in the business, I'm still surprised at what prices some early bakelite (early plastic) jewelry sells for.

Many collectors are drawn to this early form of plastic. I once sold an empty shell of a radio made of butterscotch and mauve bakelite for one thousand dollars.

FURNITURE (MARRIED AND DIVORCED)

When buying antique furniture you have to be a bit of a sleuth to determine its true age and condition. You have to check the jointing, the hardware (old or new), and the wear and tear on areas that should show hundreds of years of wear and tear.

You have to check out the cuts on the wood to see if they were made by a modern saw and planer or by a more primitive saw and plane.

Furniture, like people, can also be married or divorced. A piece is married if it finds another piece that completes or complements it even if they didn't originally start out together and a divorced piece of furniture is when one removes a rotten or damaged part from the original piece letting the remaining piece stand alone.

When selling a piece of early furniture, always look for a label or maker's mark. Some very simple looking pieces of furniture can be extremely valuable because of the designer or manufacturer.

There are many other topics I can comment on - toys, clothing, purses, compacts, glass and crystal but the universal truth is that every year billions of dollars of collectibles are undersold or thrown out because of a lack of understanding of the market and a rush to sell.

Some fakes are easy to spot, some aren't.

A bird in the hand

My days now consisted of getting up at 7 a.m. to walk my dogs down by the beach, playing a round of golf with my friends and sharing a pitcher of beer at the nineteenth hole before heading out to open the store. At least that was my life until that loving and slightly demanding wife of mine introduced me to the wonderful world of bird rescue. I'm always amazed at how she can watch Clint Eastwood blow away fifty people in a movie and not say a word but let one dog, cat, or bird get hurt and she'll walk out of the room crying "I don't know how you can sit there and watch that crap."

Marilyn's a volunteer and she has the unique ability of dragging me, kicking and screaming into her little volunteer projects. Our store takes a secondary position to the various non-paying projects she finds for both of us. One "small" project was a dinner auction for a south shore dog and cat shelter. "They need an antique evaluator,"she said "It won't take up much of your time." Two months later after running all over the city, selecting, evaluating and transporting goods and watching my home turn into a warehouse, the event finally took place. Another project of hers is the Nichoir Wild Bird Clinic and Sanctuary. I started writing this story while sitting at my computer with wet socks, pants and shoes after dropping her off at the Nichoir. What was supposed to be a simple drop off ended with me hosing down the cage floor of a crow named Manning. As I worked, Manning sat on my shoulder constantly complaining about the food and accommodations of his new resort. He was a little upset because some genius at a Golf Club and *with* a golf club, cruelly killed his mate. Probably the only birdie this character ever made. The Nichoir received a call and rushed to the location to save him from a similar fate. I discovered that crows are very family-orientated birds.

Manning did what any other concerned spouse would do and went back to the club house looking for his partner.

Working at my store, I became acquainted with various nationalities and customs of people and in time I came to understand and admire them. Working at the Nichoir opened my eyes to the amazing lives of many species of birds and helped me both understand and love them. Every volunteer becomes attached to the birds and looks forward to the day when they can be released healthy and happily back to nature.

Unfortunately, that was not possible with Manning. This funny, opinionated and totally loveable crow was just too friendly. There was a strong possibility that he would land on someone's head or shoulders and they would mistakenly assume that they were being attacked and injure or kill him. He was sent on his way to St. Jerome. A man there was under the impression he could train this rebellious character and give him a good life. I was sad when the little guy left the sanctuary in Hudson. How ironic was this? Here I was worrying about the life of this crazy little crow when not that long ago I used to hate crows. I thought of them as filthy, disease-ridden scavengers with no appealing traits whatsoever. It turns out that I had the bird brain, not Manning. When I took the time to work with crows and other birds and tried to understand them, my opinion completely changed. Manning had shown me how ignorance breeds prejudice and how our lives can be enriched if we walk around with open hearts and minds.

It's unfortunate that the Nichoir must close every winter. Like so many other great organizations, they don't have the funds to survive all year round. This wonderful establishment, which is unique in Canada, operates on donations and a yearly dinner auction. The fact that projects like the Nichoir are struggling to survive as we read stories of government corruption and corporate greed is enough to make me sick. What happens to all those sick and injured birds when they close for the winter? Someone shows up daily to check for telephone messages and attempts to place as many injured birds as they can in loving foster homes. Some die as all things must eventually die.

The truth is you can't save them all and many will die alone in the bitter cold without the attention of the many loving volunteers.

It's easy to say, as I often do to Marilyn "Honey, you can't save them all. " She just ignores me and goes about her work.

The Mallard Christmas Story

It was a cold icy Christmas day when Hudson's Le Nichoir wild bird clinic and sanctuary received a call from a concerned citizen. She had discovered a male mallard duck swimming alone in a small body of running water down a snow covered drainage ditch adjacent to her property. I was enjoying my day off, sitting by a warm fire with my feet up and enjoying a classic Christmas movie on my wide screen television when my wife Marilyn approached me. She insisted I get up, get dressed and drive her to the location without delay.

I dragged my five foot six, 250 pound couch potato body off my chair, got dressed in my Goodyear blimp down-filled jacket, put on my heavy winter boots, and headed out with my faithful but demanding companion, on a duck hunting expedition.

We found our feathered and slightly undernourished friend looking content but hungry. My wife sent me off to find nourishment in the form of a can of Niblets corn while she stayed behind to duck-sit. When I returned, the little guy ate with the gusto of Donald Duck at a corn roast. Since Le Nichoir has no winter quarters we decided, after consulting with our local expert, that it would be wiser to leave him where he was but continue monitoring and feeding him. Early every morning my wife would drag my sorry butt out of my warm comfortable house into a cold and temperamental car for a drive to Ducksville. After finding a place to park on a snow covered country street we would then head down a steep and ice covered trail to check out our new friend. I was beginning to suspect that my wife was more concerned about the "Mallard in the Pool" than the "Man in her Life." One day we arrived and he was gone. We headed for home with long faces hoping for the best but suspecting the worst.

Two weeks later on another cold miserable winter day (we seem to get a lot of those in Canada) we got an urgent call from a Mr. Ken Davy on Cameron Road in the town of Hudson. He had a Mallard duck with a beak that was frozen shut swimming in the running creek on his property. Once again we headed out on a duck hunt only to discover that it was our old friend. He was in a very small patch of water surrounded by ice.

I got the net out of the car with the noble intention of capturing our wayward buddy, thawing out his beak and giving him some temporary shelter. Murphy's Law states that it's impossible to make anything foolproof because fools are so ingenious." Ignoring this law while ratifying it, I carefully walked out onto the ice, net in hand as my wife cried out, "That ice won't hold you!" I knew that in her opinion the iceberg that sank the Titanic wasn't strong enough to support me so I ignored her pleas and continued out onto the ice. The next thing I know I was standing up to my assets in freezing water and the duck was swimming happily out of range. While I fought hypothermia my wife decided to call duck expert Lynn Miller and get her assessment of the duck's dilemma. Once more she was more concerned with the duck's frozen beak than her husband's frozen feet and snowballs.

Lynn informed her that as long as the duck didn't appear to be in any serious distress we should leave it be. It had survived this long under impossible odds and as long as we kept it well fed and monitored it daily it should be all right. She assured us that the beak would thaw out without any help from us. We then picked up a large bag of dried corn and dropped it off at Mr. Davy's home.

He promised he would feed our mutual friend daily and keep us informed of his progress. True to his word the next day we got a call informing us that the beak had defrosted and our brave and tough little Mallard was getting along fine.

The little mallard survived the winter and throughout the following summer could be seen swimming happily with a new found girlfriend. I hope she's a little easier on him than my wife is on me.

My three dogs

I couldn't write this story about my life without talking about my three dogs. They might not qualify as antiques but they sure are precious to Marilyn and me.

I remember a time when Marilyn and I went on a call to a fancy house in Westmount. As the lady of the house opened the door, my eyes were immediately enchanted by the many beautiful antiques the house contained while Marilyn's eyes were captivated with the small puppy that came running up to the door. I knew then and there where her priorities lay. All of our dogs come from animal rescues. Marilyn has this thing for strays, which is probably one of the main reasons she married me. My oldest dog Bowser came from an animal rescue that no longer exists due to financial pressures. It seems that having a big heart just isn't enough. Sometimes you need the big bank account to support it. Marilyn went to the rescue to help out one day and came home with this surprise in her arms. I took one look at this shivering and scared little golden puppy and my heart melted. I immediately took him into my arms and he immediately pissed all over me. Obviously, he had a low opinion of antique dealers or maybe it was just me. He must have been abused at one time or other because once in the house he ran under our 18th century pine table and refused to come out. We just put down paper and dog bowls for him and waited as Marilyn prayed for the dog and I prayed for my table legs. For three nights, Marilyn slept under the table at his side so he would eventually feel safe, wanted and loved and, as quoted in the bible, "On the third day he arose." This dog is so gentle that you can put a bread crumb in a child's hand and he will take it away without the child feeling a thing. Not a test I would recommend for many other dogs out there.

He's old and a little sick now. I don't think he has much more time left but this wonderful dog had a wonderful life with us. I guess that will be of some consolation when the sad day arrives.

My other dog Shanon is another story completely. Maybe I screwed up by giving him a girl's name. He can best be described as a lovable nuisance. We got him from a group I refer to as the Canine Mafia. This group of senior and middle-aged outlaw women heard a story about a dog that was left outside day and night in all kinds of weather without adequate food or water. They did some surveillance work at the location specified and verified that the story was true. They then approached the owners with an offer they could not refuse. They refused. It seems that the household was financing itself by selling drugs and the dog was their early warning system. The K-9 Mafia went into action. They dressed in black clothing and proceeded to kidnap this character in the middle of the night. The mental midgets that lived in the house failed to realize that a hungry dog can be kept quiet and led away quietly with an offer of good food. After he had spent one night at the shelter Marilyn approached me with the suggestion that we foster this fugitive until a good home could be found. She found a good home all right. It just happened to be mine.

This character is easy to recognize. When you walk up the driveway, he is the one leading the pack, jumping on your clean clothes and trying desperately to take your purse or bag out of your hands so that he can carry it proudly into the house. Once in the house, he will never leave you alone. We were having guests over for supper one day and I found him and his buddy Benny, our third dog, playing tug of war with the guest's designer jacket.

That didn't go over too well. Another time, my friend Ernie was staying overnight and we all spent the following morning chasing Shanon around the house trying to retrieve the socks, t-shirt and underwear that was logged firmly in Shanon's mouth. In the first instance we offered to pay for the designer jacket. In the second we threatened to sue Ernie for negligence resulting in dog trauma counseling and a possible stomach disorder.

That now brings me to my last dog Benny. Benny is so ugly he's cute. Only Marilyn could go to work at a bird clinic and end up treating a visually-impaired (in more ways than one) dog. I remember waking up that beautiful Saturday morning and looking forward to the golf tournament I was having later that day. With 45 minutes remaining before tee off time I got a call from Marilyn who was doing volunteer work at the Nichoir Wild Bird Rehabilitation Centre telling me that someone had dumped an undernourished dog with severe eye problems off at the clinic. I told her that unless the dog had wings and could fly I didn't want to know anything more about it. She obviously wasn't listening because she told me to forget about the tournament, pick up the dog and bring it to the vet immediately.

The fact that I was able to accomplish all this and still make the tournament in time still astonishes me. My driving skills were much more impressive than my golf skills that particular day. We picked Benny up a while later after he had recovered from some minor eye surgery and once again what was supposed to be a simple foster care ended up complicating my life. I discovered that Benny loves tea and that it is dangerous to leave your cup unattended. Now, when I try to enjoy a good cup of tea undisturbed, I find Benny fixated on my cup like a hungry breast-feeding baby at a wet tee-shirt contest. When will I ever learn that Marilyn's idea of a foster home and mine are radically different?

Now, with Bowser, Shanon and Benny, every night in my life is a three dog night.

Godmother of the K-9 Mafia

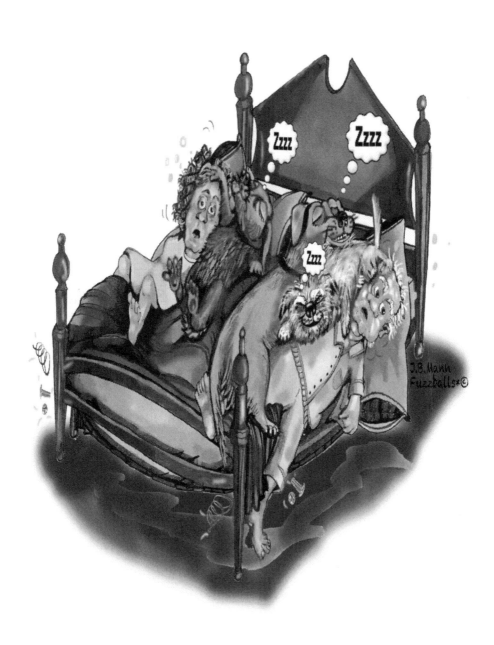

"We Really Need an Antique King Size Bed!"

Reflections

I started dealing in second hand goods in 1982 and thirty-two years later I'm still dealing in second hand goods. Thirty-two years and I still don't consider myself as an expert in the trade. There are so many different aspects to this market that even a man with the intellect of Albert Einstein couldn't possibly cover them all too any real degree of expertise. I'm no Einstein as you may have discovered. In the category of furniture you have early American, European, and Eastern, modern. Arts and crafts, art deco, Quaker, 17th -18th-19th-20th and 21st century, and every other classification under the sun. You have American pottery, English pottery, primitive pottery, toys. carpets, magazines, advertising memorabilia, cards, comics, pens, costume and gold and silver jewelry, art, militaria, porcelain, crystal, glass and every other category you can dream off.

Values are always being revised based on the latest market information and fashion. When you watch the antique road shows on television, it all seems to come so easy to the dealers delivering their opinions. What you don't see is the computer work, consultation and research that often go on behind the scenes. Prices of true antiques are not fixed and will vary from region to region and from store to store. What cost $2 at a garage sale could sell for $50 dollars at a flea market, $100 at auction, $200 at a lower end antique store or $500 at a high end shop. When I hear of a small beat up table selling for $25 at a garage sale and then for over half a million dollars at auction, I shake my head in bewilderment. Coming from a working class family, I immediately equate half a million dollars to the years of a working man's life and based on that equation, no table, not even one made by Jesus Christ, eaten at by Buddha and written on by Mohammed is worth that kind of money.

Somehow I feel that those three learned men would agree with me on that score.

Values are influenced by the elements of supply and demand, quality of workmanship and materials, auction prices, history, market manipulation and general appeal. We see manipulation of the market price in many ways. Some collectibles come out as limited editions. They might be limited to actual numbers or number of firing or manufacturing days (your guess is as good as mine on the true numbers). There are many ways to manipulate the market. One antique auctioneer of toys would create his own history by selling a toy at a very high price to a ghost bidder (everybody knows there's no such thing as a ghost) at one auction then selling the same toy at a second auction a month later chanting," What do I hear for this beautiful antique toy, I sold one just like it for $$$ at my last auction."

We see values affected by current and past history. A dress belonging to Princess Diana sold for substantially more after her unfortunate death than before it.

You would get a lot more for that old American civil war chair you own if you prove that General Ulysses Simpson Grant sat and possibly farted on it while accepting Lee's surrender at the Appomattox court house in Virginia.

Not everything that looks valuable is valuable and not everything that looks like junk is junk. Over the years I have sold marbles, fountain pens, magazines, toys, and old cans for hundreds and sometimes thousands of dollars while realizing very little money on vintage porcelain and china objects.

Today, there is a tool available that was not available when I first opened shop. The internet has proven itself a fantastic research tool and auction sites such as E-Bay have made the world accessible to collectors and sellers alike. We see some prices tumble because of it and some prices soar. People have built good careers out of buying and selling on the net for themselves and for other clients. There are some great deals out there and everybody loves a bargain.

Every time I give a talk on antiques and collectables, I end the evening by asking everyone in the audience to raise their hands if they would love to find a $1,000 antique at a garage sale for $5. With few exceptions everybody usually raises their hands. I then ask them to raise their hands if they would feel cheated if an antique dealer came to their garage sale and paid $5 for something he knew was worth $1,000. Once more everybody raises their hands. "Why the double standard?" I then ask.

Knowledge generates wealth and wealth begets power so use the tools that the Gods of cyberspace have made available to you.

Summing up

So many interesting people with interesting stories came into my life over the thirty years I've been in business. I wish I could recall all of them but I'm getting old and my brain doesn't function like it used to. Maybe one day they will discover a Viagra pill that stimulates the brain. Extended brain activity could only help me while an extended erection would probably kill me.

Among the characters, there was my Stinky Stan, the high school teacher with flip up sun glasses. He had a serious hygiene problem so I always sent Marilyn over to serve him. She's never forgiven me for that. Then was over-sexed Sandra. One day, she came into the store wishing to buy an antique lamp and asked if the wiring on the old lamp was any good. Jokingly, I replied, " Take it home, plug it in, if it blows your circuit then the wirings bad, replace it." She smiled seductively at me and said "Can I blow yours instead?" I replyed , "We're still talking about the lamp, aren't we?" My wife almost choked and the customer laughed. That quirky scense of humor of mine once again got me in trouble. Inadvertently, I had opened the floodgates.

After that incident every time she came into my store and she was a good customer who came often, it was one story about her sex life after another and they got wilder and wilder. She told me she had a grown daughter that worked with the Cirque du Soleil and I almost choked. I couldn't let my mind wander that far off base. I was a happily married man and intended to stay that way. I heard she eventually settled down with a good man. White wasn't the color of choice at that wedding.

There was Danny the cross- dresser who would come in and try on anything new in women's jewelry and Bogaloo Bob who had a thyroid problem that caused his eyes to bulge out of his head when not on medication. He always looked so surprised to see me. I hear he's fine now.

There were prima-ballerinas, movie and television actors, news broadcasters, politicians, directors. doctors, lawyers, butchers, bakers,candlestick makers and indian chiefs and I loved them all.

After thirty-two years in this business I have come to realize that I should never look for perfection in people. It doesn't exist. Look instead for a kind and loving heart, a warm smile and a little understanding.

When I leave this business, it's the people with all their small imperfections that I will miss most. Nothing is more precious to me then the memories of the lives I've touched and the lives that touched mine.

The rest will eventually become landfill.

Printed by Amazon Italia Logistica S.r.l.
Torrazza Piemonte (TO), Italy

12674623R00121